POPE

Alexander Pope was born in London in 1688. His family were
Roman Catholics and in 1700 they moved to Binfield, in Windsor
Forest, probably in conformity with anti-Catholic legislation. A
precocious boy, he was briefly at one or two Catholic schools but
mostly studied at home. When he was about twelve he had the first
of several illnesses which left him with ruined health and finally a
tubercular spine, though he continued his intensive reading and
writing. In May 1709 Pope's *Pastorals* were published, which drew
him some fame. His first major work, *An Essay on Criticism*, a bril-
liant statement of neo-classical critical principles, appeared in 1711.
In 1712 he published the first version of 'The Rape of the Lock';
this masterpiece of mock-heroic technique starts as a joke arising
from a natural incident, but contains some very powerful, even tragic,
poetry. A collection of his works, preserving all he thought worthy
of his earlier poetry, was published in 1717. For ten years Pope
worked on his translation of the *Iliad* (6 volumes, 1715–20) and for
a further three (with assistants) on the *Odyssey* (5 volumes, 1725–6).
The proceeds from his translations of Homer added considerably to
Pope's financial independence, and from 1719 he lived in Twicken-
ham, where he spent much of his time improving the garden he often
refers to in his writing. He became embroiled in the literary in-
fighting of the time, and in 1728 the first 'Dunciad' heralded his later
career as the principal satirist of the age. Associated with the satirical
passages in the 'Dunciad' are the 'Imitations of Horace', which con-
tain some of Pope's most concentrated wit and virtuoso writing in
conversational and other varied couplets. As well as being the major
English poet of the eighteenth century, Pope was also a very con-
siderable critic and a brilliant letter writer. He died in 1744.

Pope

Poems

Selected by Douglas Grant
Introduction by Angus Ross

PENGUIN BOOKS

PENGUIN BOOKS

Published by the Penguin Group
27 Wrights Lane, London W8 5TZ, England
Viking Penguin Inc., 40 West 23rd Street, New York, New York 10010, USA
Penguin Books Australia Ltd, Ringwood, Victoria, Australia
Penguin Books Canada Ltd, 2801 John Street, Markham, Ontario, Canada L3R 1B4
Penguin Books (NZ) Ltd, 182–190 Wairau Road, Auckland 10, New Zealand

Penguin Books Ltd, Registered Offices: Harmondsworth, Middlesex, England

This selection first published 1950
Reissued with a new introduction 1985
5 7 9 10 8 6

Selection copyright © Penguin Books Ltd, 1950
Introduction copyright © Penguin Books Ltd, 1971
All rights reserved

Printed and bound in Great Britain by
Cox & Wyman Ltd, Reading

Typeset in Monotype Bell
Introduction reset by Merrion Letters, London

CONTENTS

INTRODUCTION   vii

FOUR PASTORALS (1709)
    Spring   1
    Summer   4
    Autumn   7
    Winter   10

AN ESSAY ON CRITICISM (1711)   14

From WINDSOR-FOREST (1713)   36

THE RAPE OF THE LOCK (1714)   39

From THE TEMPLE OF FAME (1715)   65

ELOISA TO ABELARD (1717)   66

ELEGY TO THE MEMORY OF AN UNFORTUNATE
    LADY (1717)   78

EPISTLE TO MRS BLOUNT, WITH THE WORKS OF
    VOITURE (1712)   81

EPISTLE TO MRS TERESA BLOUNT. ON HER LEAV-
    ING THE TOWN AFTER THE CORONATION
    (1717)   84

EPISTLE TO MR JERVAS, WITH MR DRYDEN'S
    TRANSLATION OF FRESNOY'S 'ART OF
    PAINTING' (1716)   86

EPISTLE TO ROBERT EARL OF OXFORD AND EARL
    MORTIMER (1721)   89

FIVE EPITAPHS
    On the Hon. Simon Harcourt (1724)   91
    On Mrs Corbet (1730)   91
    On Sir William Trumbal (1735)   91
    On Mr Gay (1732)   92
    Intended for Sir Isaac Newton (1735)   92

ODE ON SOLITUDE (1717)   93

CONTENTS

ON SILENCE (1712)   94

THE DYING CHRISTIAN TO HIS SOUL (1736)   97

TO THE AUTHOR OF A POEM ENTITLED SUCCESSIO (1712)   98

PROLOGUE TO MR ADDISON'S TRAGEDY OF CATO (1713)   99

EPIGRAM (1738)   101

TO MRS M. B. ON HER BIRTHDAY (1727)   102

ON A CERTAIN LADY AT COURT (1751)   103

From THE ILIAD (1715–1720)
  Hector and Andromache (Book VI)   104
  Fires at Night (Book VIII)   109
  Vulcan forges a Shield for Achilles (Book XVIII)   109

From THE ODYSSEY (1725–1726)
  Ulysses and His Dog (Book XVII)   115

From THE DUNCIAD (1728, 1742)   117

From AN ESSAY ON MAN (1733–1734)   119

MORAL ESSAYS (1731–1735)
  Epistle I. Of the Knowledge and Characters of Men   130
  Epistle II. Of the Characters of Women   139
  Epistle III. Of the Use of Riches   148
  Epistle IV. Of the Use of Riches   163

EPISTLE TO DR ARBUTHNOT, *being* THE PROLOGUE TO THE SATIRES (1735)   171

From THE SATIRES AND EPISTLES OF HORACE IMITATED (1731–1738)
  To Mr Bethel (Hor. Bk. II. Sat. ii)   185
  To Lord Bolingbroke (Hor. Bk. I. Ep. ii)   191
  From To Augustus (Hor. Bk. II. Ep. i)   197

From THE EPILOGUE TO THE SATIRES (1738)   199

Index of First Lines   201

The date given after each poem is that
of its first publication

INTRODUCTION

ALEXANDER POPE was born in London in 1688, the son of elderly parents. His father, Alexander Pope, a Roman Catholic, was a merchant and linen-draper; in 1700, the family moved to Binfield in Windsor Forest where there was a Catholic colony, probably in conformity with the anti-Catholic legislation to depart from London. Pope inherited a small income from his father. A precocious boy, he was briefly at one or two Catholic schools, but mostly studied at home. When he was about twelve, he had the first of several illnesses which left him with ruined health, and finally a tubercular spine, though he continued his intensive reading and writing. He was taken up and encouraged as a prodigy by several retired men of letters in the neighbourhood, particularly William Walsh, and about 1705 he began to know something of the London writers through William Wycherley. In May 1709, Pope's *Pastorals* were published in Tonson's *Miscellany* (vol. VI) and gained him some fame. The opening of Pope's career is marked by ambition, consciousness of genius, narrow but intensive education, obtrusive help from older men of which he was vain but understandably felt imprisoning, and ill-health. The *Pastorals* are assured exercises in an almost dead poetic kind, marked by virtuoso writing. His next work, *An Essay on Criticism* (May 1711), is a brilliant epigrammatic statement of codified neo-classical critical doctrine, particularly defining the critic's social function. Pope's conception of the function of the poet and his most profound critical insights are best seen in his own practice, and conclusions based on this early work must be modified; it was, however, very influential and praised in the *Spectator* in which Pope printed 'Messiah', an imitation of Virgil's fourth 'Eclogue'.

In May 1712, Pope published the first, shorter, version of 'The Rape of the Lock', and enlarged it in 1714. This masterpiece of mock-heroic technique starts as a joke arising from an actual incident, but contains some very powerful, even tragic, poetry. It shows several themes and attitudes characteristic of Pope's later work : his attack on his society for not realizing its potentialities; his half-unwilling admiration for English opulence; his moral concern with leading the good life; and, in Belinda, his awareness of the predicament of women, creatures of nearly irresistible passion living in a man's world of reason and reputation. In 1713 Pope issued proposals for a translation of the *Iliad* (6 vols., 1715–20). For ten years he laboured on this; and for a further three (with assistants) on the *Odyssey* (5 vols., 1725–6). In 1717, he published a collection of his *Works*, preserving all he thought worthy of his earlier poetry. This includes 'Windsor-Forest', which had appeared in 1713, a topographical poem uniting natural description (he was then studying painting) with historical and social reflections; two interesting romantic poems, 'Lines to the Memory of an Unfortunate Lady', and a heroical epistle, 'Eloisa to Abelard'. It also includes translations from Chaucer and an interesting reworking, 'The House of Fame : A Vision'. This early volume shows the breadth of Pope's reading; his apprenticeship in imitation of Chaucer, Spenser, Crashaw and the Metaphysicals; and the extent of his virtuosity outside satire. The *Iliad* and *Odyssey* have great poetry in them; Pope seeks to 'realize' Homer for the contemporary reader and the labour of translation undoubtedly deepened his art. From the proceeds of the enterprise, he added considerably to his financial independence, and from 1719 lived in the pretty house at Twickenham, where he spent his life improving the garden he often refers to in his writing. At this time he was writing a fair amount of miscellaneous verse, and in 1725 published his edition of *The Works of Shakespeare*. His work is rather perfunctory, though not without insights prompted by his genius. The Homer and the Shakespeare embroiled Pope in the literary infighting of the time; and in 1728, the first 'Dunciad', with Theobald the detractor of his editorial competence as the 'hero', heralded his later career as the principal satirist of the age. Many fugitive pieces and squibs as well as later works are associated with these poems (the 'Dunciad' was reprinted with an elaborate anti-pedantic apparatus of notes as *The Dunciad Variorum* in 1729; a fourth book, *The New Dunciad*, appeared in 1742; and the poem was rewritten with Colley Cibber in Theobald's place, appearing in 1743). Pope took enormous care over the elaboration of this poem; in it the mock-heroic is more than a mere device, it becomes the vehicle for a powerful vision of English society (or at least its literary and intellectual structure). By using reminiscences of Homer, Virgil, Dante, Milton and other great constructors of visions, he unifies (more or less successfully) individual attacks on Grub Street hacks into a denunciation of the betrayal of the deepest human values. The extraordinary power of the writing allows him to imply his own view of the poet as seer, the bard who is needed to keep society healthy. The closing passage of Book IV is one of the noblest statements of this ancient and generous view of art. It gains in power, perhaps, from a prophetic sense which Pope has but never argues out, that his humanist culture is doomed by intellectual and social forces then gaining strength. The poem is eventually tragic rather than epic.

Associated with the satirical (witty and personal) passages in the 'Dunciad' are Pope's 'Imitations of Horace'. These are translations and happy adaptations to the contemporary scene of passages from Horace's *Epistles*, *Satires* and *Odes*. They are relaxed in tone, but contain some of Pope's most concentrated wit and virtuoso writing in conversational and other varied couplets. There are eleven poems of this kind. Bolingbroke gave Pope the idea, and 'The First Satire of the Second Book of Horace Imitated' appeared in February 1733. Several other works are associated with the 'Imitations'. In 1735, Pope dedicated to his dying friend 'An Epistle from Mr Pope to Dr Arbuthnot', and this was altered, given the title of 'The Prologue to the Satires' and placed at the beginning of the 'Satires' as the 'Imitations' section was called in the *Works* (1751) edited by Warburton. 'One Thousand Seven Hundred and Thirty Eight: A Dialogue something like Horace' was published in May 1738 (*Dialogue II* in July) and the title altered to 'Epilogue to the Satires' in the *Works* (8 vols., 1740), edited by Pope. Literary criticism, autobiography and politics are the themes of these poems; Pope is constantly making his judgements and justifying his positions. They do not, however, really form a homogeneous series. At times, they shade into the second great division of his later work, the poems in which he 'moralized his song' and made the positive statements of values which underlie his satire. This division comprises the 'Essay on Man' (four 'Epistles' addressed to Bolingbroke; I–III, 1733; IV, 1734) and the four poems known variously as *Epistles to Various Persons*, *Ethic Epistles* or *Moral Essays* (I, 'To Cobham: Of the Knowledge and Characters of Men', 1733–4; II, 'To a Lady [Martha Blount]: Of the Characters of Women', 1734–5; III, 'To Bathurst: Of the Use of Riches', 1732–3; IV, 'To Burlington: Of the Use of Riches' (and taste), 1731). Pope toyed with the idea that the 'Essay on Man' was the first book of a work which would include the *Epistles* as illustrations, but the idea was very tentative.

Warburton in his editing tinkered to make it clearer and more rigid. The 'Essay on Man' is a philosophical (or reflective) poem in the epistolary form, the middle style – not dramatic like *Paradise Lost* but relaxed and not rigidly argued. Books I and III are concerned with a Theodicy; that is, with what part evil plays in the world of God's dispensation and in the social order he has made for man. Whatever is, is right; man cannot know God's purposes, and cannot, therefore, complain about the existence of evil. Books II and IV are concerned with an Ethic; that is, how man must act in this world given his psychological make up. He must oppose evil. The poem makes use of traditional Christian and humanist materials : the great chain of being; the conflict of reason and passion; the argument from design. The poem is often attacked as unoriginal, but its beauty lies in the poetic tension (within the work) which Pope produces to hold the disparate, traditional materials together, since they cannot be synthesized by reason. It was attacked as unorthodox by a Swiss theologian, Crousaz, and Warburton gained his ascendancy over the old poet by coming to his rescue. Much of the defence, as well as the attack, is beside the point. The poem also serves to justify, however, the satirist's social role.

Pope also wrote influential criticism in prose that is worth studying, particularly the Prefaces to the *Iliad* and *Odyssey*. He was practically the first English writer to publish his own letters, and perhaps it was partly the novelty of the action that made necessary the complicated series of manoeuvres, false piracies and complex arrangements by which this was done between 1735 and his death. He altered the text of letters to secure 'artistic' truth, a procedure that has gained him much abuse. His letters are analyses of his own thoughts and feelings rather than accounts of his society. They were considered models of elegant writing. Later reaction against the technical domination of Pope in the poetry of the century obscured many of his noblest qualities of sympathy, humanity and passion; nineteenth-century critics were generally content to accept the stereotype of a brilliantly malicious, prosaic technician. Byron made significant objection to this faulty judgement, and in the last fifty years Pope has reappeared as the great poet he is.

ANGUS ROSS

NOTE

The text of the poems is that which William Warburton, Bishop of Gloucester, Pope's friend and executor, first published in 1751. The text of the *Iliad* and the *Odyssey* is printed from the first editions of those translations. The poems need annotation in many places, and Pope, aware of this, commented upon the obscurer passages. His notes, as far as possible, have been retained, and are distinguished with a *P*.

DOUGLAS GRANT
1950

SPRING

THE FIRST PASTORAL, OR DAMON

TO SIR WILLIAM TRUMBAL[1]

FIRST in these fields I try the sylvan strains,
Nor blush to sport on Windsor's blissful plains:
Fair Thames, flow gently from thy sacred spring,
While on thy banks Sicilian Muses sing;
Let vernal airs through trembling osiers play,
And Albion's cliffs resound the rural lay.

You that, too wise for pride, too good for pow'r,
Enjoy the glory to be great no more,
And, carrying with you all the world can boast,
To all the world illustriously are lost!
O let my Muse her slender reed inspire,
Till in your native shades you tune the lyre:
So when the Nightingale to rest removes,
The Thrush may chant to the forsaken groves,
But, charm'd to silence, listens while she sings,
And all th' aërial audience clap their wings.

Soon as the flocks shook off the nightly dews,
Two Swains, whom Love kept wakeful, and the Muse,
Pour'd o'er the whitening vale their fleecy care,
Fresh as the morn, and as the season fair:
The dawn now blushing on the mountain's side,
Thus Daphnis spoke, and Strephon thus reply'd.

DAPHNIS. Hear how the birds, on ev'ry bloomy spray,
   With joyous music wake the dawning day!
   Why sit we mute, when early linnets sing,
   When warbling Philomel salutes the spring?

1. Sir William Trumbull (1639–1716); a retired statesman and a
friend of Pope's.

Why sit we sad when Phosphor[1] shines so clear,
And lavish Nature paints the purple year?

STREPHON. Sing then, and Damon shall attend the strain,
While yon' slow oxen turn the furrow'd plain.
Here the bright crocus and blue vi'let glow,
Here western winds on breathing roses blow.
I'll stake yon' lamb, that near the fountain plays,
And from the brink his dancing shade surveys.

DAPHNIS. And I this bowl, where wanton ivy twines,
And swelling clusters bend the curling vines:
Four figures rising from the work appear,
The various seasons of the rowling year;
And what is that, which binds the radiant sky,
Where twelve fair signs in beauteous order lie?

DAMON. Then sing by turns, by turns the Muses sing,
Now hawthorns blossom, now the daisies spring,
Now leaves the trees, and flow'rs adorn the ground;
Begin, the vales shall ev'ry note rebound.

STREPHON. Inspire me, Phoebus, in my Delia's praise,
With Waller's[2] strains, or Granville's[3] moving lays!
A milk-white bull shall at your altars stand,
That threats a fight, and spurns the rising sand.

DAPHNIS. O Love! for Sylvia let me gain the prize,
And make my tongue victorious as her eyes;
No lambs or sheep for victims I'll impart,
Thy victim, Love, shall be the shepherd's heart.

STREPHON. Me gentle Delia beckons from the plain,
Then hid in shades, eludes her eager swain;
But feigns a laugh, to see me search around,
And by that laugh the willing fair is found.

1. Phosphor: the planet Venus when she appears as a morning star.
2. Edmund Waller (1606–87); the poet whose polished verses inspired Pope to imitation.
3. George Granville, Baron Lansdowne (1667–1735); poet, dramatist, and an early patron of Pope.

DAPHNIS. The sprightly Sylvia trips along the green,
She runs, but hopes she does not run unseen;
While a kind glance at her pursuer flies,
How much at variance are her feet and eyes!

STREPHON. O'er golden sands let rich Pactolus flow,
And trees weep amber on the banks of Po;
Blest Thames's shores the brightest beauties yield,
Feed here, my lambs, I'll seek no distant field.

DAPHNIS. Celestial Venus haunts Idalia's groves;
Diana Cynthus, Ceres Hybla loves;
If Windsor-shades delight the matchless maid,
Cynthus and Hybla yield to Windsor-shade.

STREPHON. All nature mourns, the skies relent in show'rs,
Hush'd are the birds, and clos'd the drooping flow'rs;
If Delia smile, the flow'rs begin to spring,
The skies to brighten, and the birds to sing.

DAPHNIS. All nature laughs, the groves are fresh and fair,
The Sun's mild lustre warms the vital air;
If Sylvia smiles, new glories gild the shore,
And vanquish'd nature seems to charm no more.

STREPHON. In spring the fields, in autumn hills I love,
At morn the plains, at noon the shady grove,
But Delia always; absent from her sight,
Nor plains at morn, nor groves at noon delight.

DAPHNIS. Sylvia's like autumn ripe, yet mild as May,
More bright than noon, yet fresh as early day;
Ev'n spring displeases, when she shines not here;
But blest with her, 'tis spring throughout the year.

STREPHON. Say, Daphnis, say, in what glad soil appears,
A wond'rous Tree that sacred Monarchs bears?[1]
Tell me but this, and I'll disclaim the prize,
And give the conquest to thy Sylvia's eyes.

---

1. An allusion to the royal oak, in which Charles II had been hid
from the pursuit after the battle of Worcester. *P.*

DAPHNIS. Nay, tell me first, in what more happy fields
   The Thistle springs, to which the Lily yields?[1]
   And then a nobler prize I will resign;
   For Sylvia, charming Sylvia shall be thine.
DAMON. Cease to contend, for, Daphnis, I decree,
   The bowl to Strephon, and the lamb to thee:
   Blest Swains, whose Nymphs in ev'ry grace excel;
   Blest Nymphs, whose Swains those graces sing so well!
   Now rise, and haste to yonder woodbine bow'rs,
   A soft retreat from sudden vernal show'rs;
   The turf with rural dainties shall be crown'd,
   While op'ning blooms diffuse their sweets around.
   For see! the gath'ring flocks to shelter tend,
   And from the Pleiads fruitful show'rs descend.

SUMMER

THE SECOND PASTORAL, OR ALEXIS

TO DR GARTH[2]

A SHEPHERD's Boy (he seeks no better name)
Led forth his flocks along the silver Thame,
Where dancing sunbeams on the waters play'd,
And verdant alders form'd a quiv'ring shade.
Soft as he mourn'd, the streams forgot to flow,
The flocks around a dumb compassion show,
The Naïads wept in ev'ry wat'ry bow'r,
And Jove consented in a silent show'r.

1. A riddle that refers to the thistle of Scotland, the device worn by
  Queen Anne, and to the lilies of France.
2. Sir Samuel Garth (1661–1719); physician, poet, and friend of
  Pope's. He wrote a fine poem, *The Dispensary*.

Accept, O GARTH! the Muse's early lays,
That adds this wreath of Ivy to thy Bays;
Hear what from Love unpractis'd hearts endure,
From Love, the sole disease thou canst not cure.

Ye shady beeches, and ye cooling streams,
Defence from Phoebus', not from Cupid's beams,
To you I mourn, nor to the deaf I sing,
The woods shall answer, and their echo ring.
The hills and rocks attend my doleful lay,
Why art thou prouder and more hard than they?
The bleating sheep with my complaints agree,
They parch'd with heat, and I inflam'd by thee.
The sultry Sirius burns the thirsty plains,
While in thy heart eternal winter reigns.

Where stray ye, Muses, in what lawn or grove,
While your Alexis pines in hopeless love?
In those fair fields where sacred Isis glides,
Or else where Cam his winding vales divides?
As in the crystal spring I view my face,
Fresh rising blushes paint the wat'ry glass;
But since those graces please thy eyes no more,
I shun the fountains which I sought before.
Once I was skill'd in ev'ry herb that grew,
And ev'ry plant that drinks the morning dew;
Ah wretched shepherd, what avails thy art,
To cure thy lambs, but not to heal thy heart!

Let other swains attend the rural care,
Feed fairer flocks, or richer fleeces sheer:
But nigh yon' mountain let me tune my lays,
Embrace my Love, and bind my brows with bays.
That flute is mine which Colin's tuneful breath
Inspir'd when living, and bequeath'd in death;
He said; 'Alexis, take this pipe, the same
That taught the groves my Rosalinda's name;'

But now the reeds shall hang on yonder tree,
For ever silent, since despis'd by thee.
Oh! were I made by some transforming pow'r
The captive bird that sings within thy bow'r!
Then might my voice thy list'ning ears employ,
And I those kisses he receives, enjoy.

   And yet my numbers please the rural throng,
Rough Satyrs dance, and Pan applauds the song:
The Nymphs, forsaking ev'ry cave and spring,
Their early fruit, and milk-white turtles bring!
Each am'rous nymph prefers her gifts in vain,
On you their gifts are all bestow'd again.
For you the swains the fairest flow'rs design,
And in one garland all their beauties join;
Accept the wreath which you deserve alone,
In whom all beauties are compriz'd in one.

   See what delights in sylvan scenes appear!
Descending Gods have found Elysium here.
In woods bright Venus with Adonis stray'd,
And chaste Diana haunts the forest-shade.
Come, lovely nymph, and bless the silent hours,
When swains from sheering seek their nightly bow'rs;
When weary reapers quit the sultry field,
And crown'd with corn their thanks to Ceres yield.
This harmless grove no lurking viper hides,
But in my breast the serpent Love abides.
Here bees from blossoms sip the rosy dew,
But your Alexis knows no sweets but you.
Oh deign to visit our forsaken seats,
The mossy fountains, and the green retreats!
Where'er you walk, cool gales shall fan the glade,
Trees, where you sit, shall crowd into a shade:
Where'er you tread, the blushing flow'rs shall rise,
And all things flourish where you turn your eyes.

Oh! how I long with you to pass my days,
Invoke the Muses, and resound your praise!
Your praise the birds shall chant in ev'ry grove,
And winds shall waft it to the pow'rs above.
But would you sing, and rival Orpheus' strain,
The wond'ring forests soon should dance again,
The moving mountains hear the pow'rful call,
And headlong streams hang list'ning in their fall!

But see, the shepherds shun the noon-day heat,
The lowing herds to murm'ring brooks retreat,
To closer shades the panting flocks remove;
Ye Gods! and is there no relief for Love?
But soon the sun with milder rays descends
To the cool ocean, where his journey ends:
On me love's fiercer flames for ever prey,
By night he scorches, as he burns by day.

AUTUMN

THE THIRD PASTORAL, OR HYLAS AND AEGON

TO MR WYCHERLEY[1]

BENEATH the shade a spreading Beech displays,
Hylas and Aegon sung their rural lays;
This mourn'd a faithless, that an absent Love,
And Delia's name and Doris' fill'd the Grove.
Ye Mantuan nymphs, your sacred succour bring;
Hylas and Aegon's rural lays I sing.

Thou, whom the Nine with Plautus' wit inspire,
The art of Terence, and Menander's fire;

1. William Wycherley (1640?–1716); the dramatist and a friend
of Pope's.

Whose sense instructs us, and whose humour charms,
Whose judgment sways us, and whose spirit warms!
Oh, skill'd in Nature! see the hearts of Swains,
Their artless passions, and their tender pains.

Now setting Phoebus shone serenely bright,
And fleecy clouds were streak'd with purple light;
When tuneful Hylas, with melodious moan,
Taught rocks to weep, and made the mountains groan.

Go, gentle gales, and bear my sighs away!
To Delia's ear the tender notes convey.
As some sad Turtle his lost love deplores,
And with deep murmurs fills the sounding shores;
Thus, far from Delia, to the winds I mourn,
Alike unheard, unpity'd, and forlorn.

Go, gentle gales, and bear my sighs along!
For her, the feather'd choirs neglect their song:
For her, the limes their pleasing shades deny;
For her, the lilies hang their heads and die.
Ye flow'rs that droop, forsaken by the spring,
Ye birds that, left by summer, cease to sing,
Ye trees that fade when autumn-heats remove,
Say, is not absence death to those who love?

Go, gentle gales, and bear my sighs away!
Curs'd be the fields that cause my Delia's stay;
Fade ev'ry blossom, wither ev'ry tree,
Die ev'ry flow'r, and perish all, but she.
What have I said? Where'er my Delia flies,
Let spring attend, and sudden flow'rs arise;
Let op'ning roses knotted oaks adorn,
And liquid amber drop from ev'ry thorn.

Go, gentle gales, and bear my sighs along!
The birds shall cease to tune their ev'ning song,
The winds to breathe, the waving woods to move,
And streams to murmur, e'er I cease to love.

Not bubbling fountains to the thirsty swain,
Not balmy sleep to lab'rers faint with pain,
Not show'rs to larks, or sunshine to the bee,
Are half so charming as thy sight to me.

   Go, gentle gales, and bear my sighs away!
Come, Delia, come; ah, why this long delay?
Thro' rocks and caves the name of Delia sounds,
Delia, each cave and echoing rock rebounds.
Ye pow'rs, what pleasing frenzy soothes my mind!
Do lovers dream, or is my Delia kind?
She comes, my Delia comes! – Now cease my lay,
And cease, ye gales, to bear my sighs away!

   Next Aegon sung, while Windsor groves admir'd;
Rehearse, ye Muses, what yourselves inspir'd.

   Resound, ye hills, resound my mournful strain!
Of perjur'd Doris, dying I complain:
Here, where the mountains, less'ning as they rise,
Lose the low vales, and steal into the skies:
While lab'ring oxen, spent with toil and heat,
In their loose traces from the field retreat:
While curling smokes from village tôps are seen,
And the fleet shades glide o'er the dusky green.

   Resound, ye hills, resound my mournful lay!
Beneath yon' poplar oft we past the day:
Oft' on the rind I carv'd her am'rous vows,
While she with garlands hung the bending boughs:
The garlands fade, the vows are worn away;
So dies her love, and so my hopes decay.

   Resound, ye hills, resound my mournful strain!
Now bright Arcturus glads the teeming grain,
Now golden fruits on loaded branches shine,
And grateful clusters swell with floods of wine;
Now blushing berries paint the yellow grove;
Just Gods! shall all things yield returns but love?

Resound, ye hills, resound my mournful lay!
The shepherds cry, 'Thy flocks are left a prey' –
Ah! what avails it me, the flocks to keep,
Who lost my heart while I preserv'd my sheep.
Pan came, and ask'd, what magic caus'd my smart,
Or what ill eyes malignant glances dart?
What eyes but hers, alas, have pow'r to move!
And is there magic but what dwells in love!

Resound, ye hills, resound my mournful strains!
I'll fly from shepherds, flocks, and flow'ry plains.
From shepherds, flocks, and plains, I may remove,
Forsake mankind, and all the world – but love!
I know thee, Love! on foreign mountains bred,
Wolves gave thee suck, and savage tigers fed.
Thou wert from Aetna's burning entrails torn,
Got by fierce whirlwinds, and in thunder born!

Resound, ye hills, resound my mournful lay!
Farewell, ye woods; adieu, the light of day!
One leap from yonder cliff shall end my pains;
No more, ye hills, no more resound my strains!

Thus sung the shepherds till th' approach of night,
The skies yet blushing with departing light,
When falling dews with spangles deck'd the glade,
And the low sun had lengthen'd ev'ry shade.

WINTER

THE FOURTH PASTORAL, OR DAPHNE
TO THE MEMORY OF MRS TEMPEST[1]

LYCIDAS. Thyrsis, the music of that murm'ring spring
Is not so mournful as the strains you sing.

1. Mrs Tempest (d. 1703) was the friend of Pope's early friend and
adviser William Walsh (1663–1708), the critic.

Nor rivers winding thro' the vales below,
So sweetly warble, or so smoothly flow.
Now sleeping flocks on their soft fleeces lie,
The moon, serene in glory, mounts the sky,
While silent birds forget their tuneful lays,
Oh sing of Daphne's fate, and Daphne's praise!

THYRSIS. Behold the groves that shine with silver frost,
Their beauty wither'd, and their verdure lost.
Here shall I try the sweet Alexis' strain,
That call'd the list'ning Dryads to the plain?
Thames heard the numbers as he flow'd along,
And bade his willows learn the moving song.

LYCIDAS. So may kind rains their vital moisture yield,
And swell the future harvest of the field.
Begin; this charge the dying Daphne gave,
And said, 'Ye shepherds, sing around my grave!'
Sing, while beside the shaded tomb I mourn,
And with fresh bays her rural shrine adorn.

THYRSIS. Ye gentle Muses, leave your crystal spring,
Let Nymphs and Sylvans cypress garlands bring;
Ye weeping Loves, the stream with myrtles hide,
And break your bows, as when Adonis died;
And with your golden darts, now useless grown,
Inscribe a verse on this relenting stone:
'Let nature change, let heav'n and earth deplore,
Fair Daphne's dead, and love is now no more!'
'Tis done, and nature's various charms decay;
See gloomy clouds obscure the chearful day!
Now hung with pearls the dropping trees appear,
Their faded honours scatter'd on her bier.
See, where on earth the flow'ry glories lie,
With her they flourish'd, and with her they die.
Ah what avail the beauties Nature wore?
Fair Daphne's dead, and beauty is no more!

11

For her the flocks refuse their verdant food,
The thirsty heifers shun the gliding flood,
The silver swans her hapless fate bemoan,
In notes more sad than when they sing their own;
In hollow caves sweet Echo silent lies,
Silent, or only to her name replies;
Her name with pleasure once she taught the shore;
Now Daphne's dead, and pleasure is no more!

No grateful dews descend from ev'ning skies,
Nor morning odours from the flow'rs arise;
No rich perfumes refresh the fruitful field,
Nor fragrant herbs their native incense yield.
The balmy Zephyrs, silent since her death,
Lament the ceasing of a sweeter breath;
Th' industrious bees neglect their golden store!
Fair Daphne's dead, and sweetness is no more!

No more the mounting larks, while Daphne sings,
Shall list'ning in mid air suspend their wings;
No more the birds shall imitate her lays,
Or hush'd with wonder, hearken from the sprays:
No more the streams their murmurs shall forbear,
A sweeter music than their own to hear,
But tell the reeds, and tell the vocal shore,
Fair Daphne's dead, and music is no more!

Her fate is whisper'd by the gentle breeze,
And told in sighs to all the trembling trees;
The trembling trees, in ev'ry plain and wood,
Her fate remurmur to the silver flood;
The silver flood, so lately calm, appears
Swell'd with new passion, and o'erflows with tears;
The winds, and trees, and floods her death deplore,
Daphne, our grief! our glory now no more!

But see! where Daphne wond'ring mounts on high
Above the clouds, above the starry sky!

Eternal beauties grace the shining scene,
Fields ever fresh, and groves for ever green!
There while you rest in Amaranthine bow'rs,
Or from those meads select unfading flow'rs,
Behold us kindly, who your name implore,
Daphne, our Goddess, and our grief no more!

LYCIDAS. How all things listen, while thy Muse com-
    plains!
Such silence waits on Philomela's strains,
In some still ev'ning, when the whisp'ring breeze
Pants on the leaves, and dies upon the trees.
To thee, bright goddess, oft a lamb shall bleed,
If teeming ewes increase my fleecy breed.
While plants their shade, or flow'rs their odours give,
Thy name, thy honour, and thy praise shall live!

THYRSIS. But see, Orion sheds unwholesome dews;
Arise, the pines a noxious shade diffuse;
Sharp Boreas blows, and Nature feels decay,
Time conquers all, and we must Time obey.
Adieu, ye vales, ye mountains, streams, and groves;
Adieu, ye shepherds' rural lays, and loves;
Adieu, my flocks; farewell, ye sylvan crew;
Daphne, farewell; and all the world, adieu!

AN ESSAY ON CRITICISM

I

'Tɪs hard to say, if greater want of skill
Appear in writing or in judging ill;
But, of the two, less dang'rous is th' offence
To tire our patience, than mislead our sense.
Some few in that, but numbers err in this;
Ten censure wrong for one who writes amiss;
A fool might once himself alone expose,
Now one in verse makes many more in prose.

'Tis with our judgments as our watches, none
Go just alike, yet each believes his own.
In Poets as true genius is but rare,
True Taste as seldom is the Critic's share;
Both must alike from Heav'n derive their light,
These born to judge, as well as those to write.
Let such teach others who themselves excel,
And censure freely who have written well.
Authors are partial to their wit, 'tis true,
But are not Critics to their judgment too?

Yet if we look more closely, we shall find
Most have the seeds of judgment in their mind:
Nature affords at least a glimm'ring light;
The lines, tho' touch'd but faintly, are drawn right.
But as the slightest sketch, if justly trac'd,
Is by ill-colouring but the more disgrac'd,
So by false learning is good sense defac'd:
Some are bewilder'd in the maze of schools,
And some made coxcombs Nature meant but fools.
In search of wit these lose their common sense,
And then turn Critics in their own defence:
Each burns alike, who can, or cannot write,
Or with a Rival's, or an Eunuch's spite.

14

All fools have still an itching to deride,
And fain would be upon the laughing side.
If Maevius scribble in Apollo's spight
There are who judge still worse than he can write.

    Some have at first for Wits, then Poets past,
Turn'd Critics next, and prov'd plain fools at last.
Some neither can for Wits nor Critics pass,
As heavy mules are neither horse nor ass.
Those half-learn'd witlings, numerous in our isle,
As half-form'd insects on the banks of Nile;
Unfinish'd things, one knows not what to call,
Their generation's so equivocal:
To tell 'em would a hundred tongues require,
Or one vain wit's, that might a hundred tire.

    But you who seek to give and merit fame,
And justly bear a Critic's noble name,
Be sure yourself and your own reach to know,
How far your genius, taste, and learning go;
Launch not beyond your depth, but be discreet,
And mark that point where sense and dulness meet.

    Nature to all things fix'd the limits fit,
And wisely curb'd proud man's pretending wit.
As on the land while here the ocean gains,
In other parts it leaves wide sandy plains;
Thus in the soul while memory prevails,
The solid pow'r of understanding fails;
Where beams of warm imagination play,
The memory's soft figures melt away.
One science only will one genius fit,
So vast is art, so narrow human wit:
Not only bounded to peculiar arts,
But oft in those confin'd to single parts.
Like Kings, we lose the conquests gain'd before,
By vain ambition still to make them more:

Each might his sev'ral province well command,
Would all but stoop to what they understand.

First follow Nature, and your judgment frame
By her just standard, which is still the same:
Unerring NATURE, still divinely bright,
One clear, unchang'd, and universal light,
Life, force, and beauty, must to all impart,
At once the source, and end, and test of Art.
Art from that fund each just supply provides;
Works without show, and without pomp presides;
In some fair body thus th' informing soul
With spirits feeds, with vigour fills the whole,
Each motion guides, and ev'ry nerve sustains,
Itself unseen, but in th' effects remains.
Some, to whom Heav'n in wit has been profuse,
Want as much more to turn it to its use;
For wit and judgment often are at strife,
Tho' meant each other's aid, like man and wife.
'Tis more to guide, than spur the Muse's steed;
Restrain his fury, than provoke his speed;
The winged courser, like a gen'rous horse,
Shows most true mettle when you check his course.

Those RULES of old discover'd, not devis'd,
Are Nature still, but Nature methodiz'd;
Nature, like Liberty, is but restrain'd
By the same Laws which first herself ordain'd.

Hear how learn'd Greece her useful rules indites,
When to repress, and when indulge our flights:
High on Parnassus' top her sons she show'd,
And pointed out those arduous paths they trod;
Held from afar, aloft, th' immortal prize,
And urg'd the rest by equal steps to rise.
Just precepts thus from great examples giv'n,
She drew from them what they deriv'd from Heav'n.

The gen'rous Critic fann'd the Poet's fire,
And taught the world with Reason to admire.
Then Criticism the Muse's handmaid prov'd,
To dress her charms, and make her more belov'd:
But following wits from that intention stray'd,
Who could not win the mistress, woo'd the maid;
Against the Poets their own arms they turn'd,
Sure to hate most the men from whom they learn'd.
So modern 'Pothecaries, taught the art,
By Doctor's bills to play the Doctor's part,
Bold in the practice of mistaken rules,
Prescribe, apply, and call their masters fools.
Some on the leaves of ancient authors prey,
Nor time nor moths e'er spoil'd so much as they.
Some drily plain, without invention's aid,
Write dull receipts, how poems may be made.
These leave the sense, their learning to display,
And those explain the meaning quite away.

   You, then, whose judgment the right course would
     steer,
Know well each ANCIENT's proper character;
His Fable, Subject, scope in ev'ry page;
Religion, Country, genius of his Age;
Without all these at once before your eyes,
Cavil you may, but never criticize.
Be Homer's works your study and delight,
Read them by day, and meditate by night;
Thence form your judgment, thence your maxims bring,
And trace the Muses upward to their spring.
Still with itself compar'd, his text peruse;
And let your comment be the Mantuan Muse.

   When first young Maro[1] in his boundless mind,
A work t' outlast immortal Rome design'd,

1. Virgil – whose family name was Maro – (70–19 B.C.); the Roman
poet. His birth-place was Mantua.

Perhaps he seem'd above the Critic's law,
And but from Nature's fountain scorn'd to draw:
But when t' examine ev'ry part he came,
Nature and Homer were, he found, the same.
Convinc'd, amaz'd, he checks the bold design,
And rules as strict his labour'd work confine,
As if the Stagirite[1] o'erlook'd each line.
Learn hence for ancient rules a just esteem;
To copy nature is to copy them.

   Some beauties yet no Precepts can declare,
For there's a happiness as well as care.
Music resembles Poetry, in each
Are nameless graces which no methods teach,
And which a master-hand alone can reach.
If, where the rules not far enough extend,
(Since rules were made but to promote their end)
Some lucky licence answer to the full
Th' intent propos'd, that licence is a rule.
Thus Pegasus, a nearer way to take,
May boldly deviate from the common track;
From vulgar bounds with brave disorder part,
And snatch a grace beyond the reach of art,
Which without passing through the judgment, gains
The heart, and all its end at once attains.
In prospects thus, some objects please our eyes,
Which out of nature's common order rise,
The shapeless rock, or hanging precipice.
Great Wits sometimes may gloriously offend,
And rise to faults true Critics dare not mend,
But tho' the Ancients thus their rules invade,
(As Kings dispense with laws themselves have made)
Moderns, beware! or if you must offend
Against the precept, ne'er transgress its End;

---

1. Aristotle – who was born at Stagyra – (384–22 B.C.); the great Greek philosopher who wrote upon the art of poetry.

Let it be seldom, and compell'd by need,
And have, at least, their precedent to plead.
The Critic else proceeds without remorse,
Seizes your fame, and puts his laws in force.

I know there are, to whose presumptuous thoughts,
Those freer beauties, ev'n in them, seem faults.
Some figures monstrous and mis-shaped appear,
Consider'd singly, or beheld too near,
Which, but proportion'd to their light, or place,
Due distance reconciles to form and grace.
A prudent chief not always must display
His pow'rs in equal ranks, and fair array,
But with th' occasion and the place comply,
Conceal his force, nay seem sometimes to fly.
Those oft are stratagems which errors seem,
Nor is it Homer nods, but we that dream.

Still green with bays each ancient Altar stands,
Above the reach of sacrilegious hands;
Secure from Flames, from Envy's fiercer rage,
Destructive War, and all-involving Age.
See from each clime the learn'd their incense bring!
Hear, in all tongues consenting Paeans ring!
In praise so just let ev'ry voice be join'd,
And fill the gen'ral chorus of mankind.
Hail, Bards triumphant! born in happier days;
Immortal heirs of universal praise!
Whose honours with increase of ages grow,
As streams roll down, enlarging as they flow;
Nations unborn your mighty names shall sound,
And worlds applaud that must not yet be found!
O may some spark of your celestial fire,
The last, the meanest of your sons inspire,
(That on weak wings, from far, pursues your flights;
Glows while he reads, but trembles as he writes)

To teach vain Wits a science little known,
T' admire superior sense, and doubt their own!

II

OF all the causes which conspire to blind
Man's erring judgment, and misguide the mind,
What the weak head with strongest bias rules,
Is *Pride*, the never-failing vice of fools.
Whatever Nature has in worth deny'd,
She gives in large recruits of needful Pride;
For as in bodies, thus in souls, we find
What wants in blood and spirits, swell'd with
        wind:
Pride, where Wit fails, steps in to our defence,
And fills up all the mighty Void of sense:
If once right reason drives that cloud away,
Truth breaks upon us with resistless day.
Trust not yourself; but your defects to know,
Make use of ev'ry friend – and ev'ry foe.

A *little learning* is a dang'rous thing;
Drink deep, or taste not the Pierian spring:
There shallow draughts intoxicate the brain,
And drinking largely sobers us again.
Fir'd at first sight with what the Muse imparts,
In fearless youth we tempt the heights of Arts,
While from the bounded level of our mind,
Short views we take, nor see the lengths behind;
But, more advanc'd, behold with strange surprise,
New distant scenes of endless science rise!
So pleas'd at first the tow'ring Alps we try,
Mount o'er the vales, and seem to tread the sky,
Th' eternal snows appear already past,
And the first clouds and mountains seem the last:

But, those attain'd, we tremble to survey
The growing labours of the lengthen'd way,
Th' increasing prospect tires our wand'ring eyes,
Hills peep o'er hills, and Alps on Alps arise!
    A perfect Judge will read each work of Wit
With the same spirit that its author writ:
Survey the WHOLE, nor seek slight faults to find
Where nature moves, and rapture warms the mind;
Nor lose, for that malignant dull delight,
The gen'rous pleasure to be charm'd with wit.
But in such lays as neither ebb nor flow,
Correctly cold, and regularly low,
That shunning faults, one quiet tenor keep,
We cannot blame indeed – but we may sleep.
In Wit, as Nature, what affects our hearts
Is not th' exactness of peculiar parts;
'Tis not a lip, or eye, we beauty call,
But the joint force and full result of all.
Thus when we view some well-proportion'd dome,
(The world's just wonder, and ev'n thine, O Rome!)
No single parts unequally surprise,
All comes united to th' admiring eyes;
No monstrous height, or breadth, or length appear;
The Whole at once is bold, and regular.
    Whoever thinks a faultless piece to see,
Thinks what ne'er was, nor is, nor e'er shall be.
In ev'ry work regard the writer's End,
Since none can compass more than they intend;
And if the means be just, the conduct true,
Applause, in spight of trivial faults, is due.
As men of breeding, sometimes men of wit,
T' avoid great errors, must the less commit:
Neglect the rules each verbal Critic lays,
For not to know some trifles is a praise.

Most Critics, fond of some subservient art,
Still make the Whole depend upon a Part:
They talk of principles, but notions prize,
And all to one lov'd Folly sacrifice.

       .   .   .

Some to *Conceit* alone their taste confine,
And glitt'ring thoughts struck out at ev'ry line;
Pleas'd with a work where nothing's just or fit;
One glaring Chaos and wild heap of wit.
Poets, like painters, thus, unskill'd to trace
The naked nature and the living grace,
With gold and jewels cover ev'ry part,
And hide with ornaments their want of art.
True Wit is Nature to advantage dress'd;
What oft was thought, but ne'er so well express'd;
Something, whose truth convinc'd at sight we find,
That gives us back the image of our mind.
As shades more sweetly recommend the light,
So modest plainness sets off sprightly wit.
For works may have more wit than does 'em good,
As bodies perish through excess of blood.
  Others for *Language* all their care express,
And value books, as women men, for dress:
Their praise is still, – 'The Style is excellent;'
The Sense, they humbly take upon content.
Words are like leaves, and where they most abound,
Much fruit of sense beneath is rarely found.
False Eloquence, like the prismatic glass,
Its gaudy colours spreads on ev'ry place;
The face of Nature we no more survey,
All glares alike, without distinction gay;
But true Expression, like th' unchanging Sun,
Clears, and improves whate'er it shines upon;
It gilds all objects, but it alters none.

22

Expression is the dress of thought, and still
Appears more decent, as more suitable;
A vile conceit in pompous words express'd,
Is like a clown in regal purple dress'd:
For diff'rent styles with diff'rent subjects sort,
As sev'ral garbs with country, town, and court.
Some by old words to fame have made pretence,
Ancients in phrase, mere moderns in their sense;
Such labour'd nothings, in so strange a style,
Amaze th' unlearn'd, and make the learned smile.

. . . . . .

In words, as fashions, the same rule will hold;
Alike fantastic, if too new, or old:
Be not the first by whom the new are try'd,
Nor yet the last to lay the old aside.
  But most by Numbers judge a Poet's song;
And smooth or rough, with them, is right or wrong:
In the bright Muse, tho' thousand charms conspire,
Her voice is all these tuneful fools admire;
Who haunt Parnassus but to please their ear, ⎫
Not mend their minds; as some to church repair, ⎬
Not for the doctrine, but the music there. ⎭
These equal syllables alone require,
Tho' oft the ear the open vowels tire;
While expletives their feeble aid do join,
And ten low words oft creep in one dull line:
While they ring round the same unvary'd chimes,
With sure returns of still expected rhymes;
Where'er you find 'the cooling western breeze,'
In the next line, it 'whispers through the trees:'
If crystal streams 'with pleasing murmurs creep',
The reader's threaten'd (not in vain) with 'sleep':
Then, at the last and only couplet fraught
With some unmeaning thing they call a thought,

23

A needless Alexandrine ends the song,
That, like a wounded snake, drags its slow length along.
Leave such to tune their own dull rhymes, and know
What's roundly smooth, or languishingly slow;
And praise the easy vigour of a line,
Where Denham's[1] strength and Waller's[2] sweetness
    join.
True ease in writing comes from art, not chance,
As those move easiest who have learn'd to dance.
'Tis not enough no harshness gives offence,
The sound must seem an Echo to the sense;
Soft is the strain when Zephyr gently blows,
And the smooth stream in smoother numbers flows:
But when loud surges lash the sounding shore,
The hoarse, rough verse should like the torrent roar.
When Ajax strives some rock's vast weight to throw,
The line too labours, and the words move slow;
Not so, when swift Camilla scours the plain,
Flies o'er th' unbending corn, and skims along the main.
Hear how Timotheus' vary'd lays surprize,[3]
And bid alternate passions fall and rise!
While at each change, the son of Lybian Jove
Now burns with glory, and then melts with love;
Now his fierce eyes with sparkling fury glow,
Now sighs steal out, and tears begin to flow:
Persians and Greeks like turns of nature found,
And the World's victor stood subdued by Sound!
The power of Music all our hearts allow,
And what Timotheus was, is DRYDEN now.

1. Sir John Denham (1615–69); the poet who wrote the famous
descriptive poem, *Cooper's Hill.*
2. See p. 2, n. 2.
3. Timotheus is the musician described playing before Alexander the
Great in John Dryden's ode, *Alexander's Feast.*

Avoid Extremes; and shun the fault of such
Who still are pleas'd too little or too much.
At ev'ry trifle scorn to take offence:
That always shows great pride, or little sense;
Those heads, as stomachs, are not sure the best
Which nauseate all, and nothing can digest.
Yet let not each gay Turn thy rapture move,
For fools admire, but men of sense approve:
As things seem large which we through mists descry,
Dulness is ever apt to magnify.

Some foreign writers, some our own despise;
The Ancients only, or the Moderns prize.
Thus Wit, like Faith, by each man is apply'd
To one small sect, and all are damn'd beside.
Meanly they seek the blessing to confine,
And force that sun but on a part to shine,
Which not alone the southern wit sublimes,
But ripens spirits in cold northern climes;
Which from the first has shone on ages past,
Enlights the present, and shall warm the last;
Tho' each may feel increases and decays,
And see now clearer and now darker days.
Regard not then if Wit be old or new,
But blame the false, and value still the true.

Some ne'er advance a Judgment of their own,
But catch the spreading notion of the Town;
They reason and conclude by precedent,
And own stale nonsense which they ne'er invent.
Some judge of authors' names, not works, and then
Nor praise nor blame the writings, but the men.
Of all this servile herd, the worst is he
That in proud dulness joins with Quality;
A constant Critic at the great man's board,
To fetch and carry nonsense for my Lord.

What woful stuff this madrigal would be,
In some starv'd hackney sonneteer, or me?
But let a Lord once own the happy lines,
How the wit brightens! how the stile refines!
Before his sacred name flies ev'ry fault,
And each exalted stanza teems with thought!
  The Vulgar thus through Imitation err;
As oft the Learn'd by being singular:
So much they scorn the crowd, that if the throng
By chance go right, they purposely go wrong:
So Schismatics the plain believers quit,
And are but damn'd for having too much wit.
Some praise at morning what they blame at night,
But always think the last opinion right.
A Muse by these is like a mistress us'd,
This hour she's idoliz'd, the next abus'd;
While their weak heads, like towns unfortify'd,
'Twixt sense and nonsense daily change their side.
Ask them the cause; they're wiser still, they say;
And still to-morrow's wiser than to-day.
We think our fathers fools, so wise we grow;
Our wiser sons, no doubt, will think us so.
Once School-divines this zealous isle o'erspread;
Who knew most Sentences, was deepest read;
Faith, Gospel, all, seem'd made to be disputed,
And none had sense enough to be confuted:
Scotists and Thomists, now, in peace remain,[1]
Amidst their kindred cobwebs in Duck-lane.[2]
If Faith itself has diff'rent dresses worn,
What wonder modes in Wit should take their turn?

1. Two differing theological schools headed by St Thomas Aquinas
   (1225–74) and Duns Scotus (1265?–1308?).
2. A place where old and second-hand books were sold formerly, near
   Smithfield. *P.*

Oft, leaving what is natural and fit,
The current folly proves the ready wit,
And authors think their reputation safe,
Which lives as long as fools are pleas'd to laugh.
    Some valuing those of their own side or mind,
Still make themselves the measure of mankind:
Fondly we think we honour merit then,
When we but praise ourselves in other men.
Parties in Wit attend on those of State,
And public faction doubles private hate.
Pride, Malice, Folly, against Dryden rose,
In various shapes of Parsons, Critics, Beaus;
But sense surviv'd, when merry jests were past;
For rising merit will buoy up at last.
Might he return, and bless once more our eyes,
New Blackmores and new Milbourns must arise:[1]
Nay, should great Homer lift his awful head,
Zoilus[2] again would start up from the dead.
Envy will merit, as its shade, pursue,
But like a shadow, proves the substance true;
For envy'd Wit, like Sol eclips'd, makes known
Th' opposing body's grossness, not its own.
When first that sun too pow'rful beams displays,
It draws up vapours which obscure its rays;
But ev'n those clouds at last adorn its way,
Reflect new glories, and augment the day.
    Be thou the first true merit to befriend;
His praise is lost, who stays 'till all commend.
Short is the date, alas, of modern rhymes,
And 'tis but just to let them live betimes.

1. Sir Richard Blackmore (d. 1729); physician. The Rev. Luke Milbourne (1649–1720). Both these were detractors of Dryden and dull poets.
2. Zoilus; a malignant critic of Homer.

No longer now that golden age appears,
When Patriarch-wits surviv'd a thousand years:
Now length of Fame (our second life) is lost,
And bare threescore is all ev'n that can boast;
Our sons their fathers' failing language see,
And such as Chaucer is, shall Dryden be.
So when the faithful pencil has design'd
Some bright Idea of the master's mind,
Where a new world leaps out at his command,
And ready Nature waits upon his hand;
When the ripe colours soften and unite,
And sweetly melt into just shade and light;
When mellowing years their full perfection give,
And each bold figure just begins to live,
The treach'rous colours the fair art betray,
And all the bright creation fades away!

Unhappy Wit, like most mistaken things,
Atones not for that envy which it brings.
In youth alone its empty praise we boast,
But soon the short-liv'd vanity is lost:
Like some fair flow'r the early spring supplies,
That gaily blooms, but ev'n in blooming dies.
What is this Wit, which must our cares employ?
The owner's wife, that other men enjoy;
Then most our trouble still when most admir'd,
And still the more we give, the more requir'd;
Whose fame with pains we guard, but lose with ease,
Sure some to vex, but never all to please;
'Tis what the vicious fear, the virtuous shun,
By fools 'tis hated, and by knaves undone!

If Wit so much from Ign'rance undergo,
Ah let not Learning too commence its foe!
Of old, those met rewards who could excel,
And such were prais'd who but endeavour'd well:

Though triumphs were to gen'rals only due,
Crowns were reserv'd to grace the soldiers too.
Now, they who reach Parnassus' lofty crown,
Employ their pains to spurn some others down;
And while self-love each jealous writer rules,
Contending wits become the sport of fools:
But still the worst with most regret commend,
For each ill Author is as bad a Friend.
To what base ends, and by what abject ways,
Are mortals urg'd through sacred lust of praise!
Ah ne'er so dire a thirst of glory boast,
Nor in the Critic let the Man be lost.
Good-nature and good-sense must ever join;
To err is human, to forgive, divine.

But if in noble minds some dregs remain,
Not yet purg'd off, of spleen and sour disdain;
Discharge that rage on more provoking crimes,
Nor fear a dearth in these flagitious times.
No pardon vile Obscenity should find,
Though wit and art conspire to move your mind;
But Dulness with Obscenity must prove
As shameful sure as Impotence in love.
In the fat age of pleasure, wealth, and ease,
Sprung the rank weed, and thriv'd with large increase:
When love was all an easy Monarch's care;[1]
Seldom at council, never in a war:
Jilts rul'd the state, and statesmen farces writ;
Nay, wits had pensions, and young Lords had wit;
The Fair sat panting at a Courtier's play,
And not a Mask went unimprov'd away:
The modest fan was lifted up no more,
And Virgins smil'd at what they blush'd before.

---

1. A reference to the times following upon the restoration of
Charles II to the throne in 1660.

The following license of a Foreign reign
Did all the dregs of bold Socinus[1] drain;
Then unbelieving Priests reform'd the nation,
And taught more pleasant methods of salvation;
Where Heav'n's free subjects might their rights dispute,
Lest God himself should seem too absolute:
Pulpits their sacred satire learn'd to spare,
And Vice admir'd to find a flatt'rer there!
Encourag'd thus, Wit's Titans brav'd the skies,
And the press groan'd with licens'd blasphemies.
These monsters, Critics! with your darts engage,
Here point your thunder, and exhaust your rage!
Yet shun their fault, who, scandalously nice,
Will needs mistake an author into vice;
All seems infected that th' infected spy,
As all looks yellow to the jaundic'd eye.

III

LEARN, then, what MORALS Critics ought to show,
For 'tis but half a Judge's task to know.
'Tis not enough, taste, judgment, learning join;
In all you speak, let truth and candour shine:
That not alone what to your sense is due
All may allow; but seek your friendship too.

Be silent always, when you doubt your sense;
And speak, tho' sure, with seeming diffidence:
Some positive, persisting fops we know,
Who, if once wrong, will needs be always so;
But you, with pleasure own your errors past,
And make each day a Critique on the last.

'Tis not enough your counsel still be true;
Blunt truths more mischief than nice falsehoods do;

1. The propounder of the heresy called Socinianism.

Men must be taught as if you taught them not,
And things unknown propos'd as things forgot.
Without Good-Breeding, truth is disapprov'd;
That only makes superior sense belov'd.
  Be niggards of advice on no pretence;
For the worst avarice is that of sense.
With mean complaisance ne'er betray your trust,
Nor be so civil as to prove unjust.
Fear not the anger of the wise to raise;
Those best can bear reproof, who merit praise.
  'Twere well might Critics still this freedom take,
But Appius reddens at each word you speak,
And stares, tremendous, with a threat'ning eye,
Like some fierce Tyrant in old tapestry.
Fear most to tax an Honourable fool,
Whose right it is, uncensur'd, to be dull;
Such, without wit, are Poets when they please,
As without learning they can take Degrees.
Leave dang'rous truths to unsuccessful Satires,
And flattery to fulsome Dedicators,
Whom, when they praise, the world believes no more,
Than when they promise to give scribbling o'er.
'Tis best sometimes your censure to restrain,
And charitably let the dull be vain:
Your silence there is better than your spite,
For who can rail so long as they can write?
Still humming on, their drouzy course they keep,
And lash'd so long, like tops, are lash'd asleep.
False steps but help them to renew the race,
As, after stumbling, Jades will mend their pace.
What crowds of these, impeniently bold,
In sounds and jingling syllables grown old,
Still run on Poets, in a raging vein,
Ev'n to the dregs and squeezings of the brain,

Strain out the last dull droppings of their sense,
And rhyme with all the rage of Impotence!
    Such shameless Bards we have; and yet 'tis true,
There are as mad, abandon'd Critics too.
The bookful blockhead, ignorantly read,
With loads of learned lumber in his head,
With his own tongue still edifies his ears,
And always list'ning to himself appears.
All books he reads, and all he reads assails,
From Dryden's Fables down to Durfey's Tales.[1]
With him most authors steal their works, or buy:
Garth did not write his own Dispensary[2]
Name a new play, and he's the Poet's friend,
Nay, show'd his faults – but when would Poets mend?
No place so sacred from such fops is barr'd,
Nor is Paul's church more safe than Paul's church yard.[3]
Nay, fly to Altars; there they'll talk you dead:
For Fools rush in where Angels fear to tread.
Distrustful sense with modest caution speaks, ⎫
It still looks home, and short excursions makes; ⎬
But rattling nonsense in full vollies breaks, ⎭
And never shock'd, and never turn'd aside,
Bursts out, resistless, with a thund'ring tide.

    But where's the man, who counsel can bestow,
Still pleas'd to teach, and yet not proud to know?
Unbiass'd, or by favour, or by spite;
Not dully prepossess'd, nor blindly right;
Tho' learn'd, well-bred; and tho' well-bred, sincere;
Modestly bold, and humanly severe:
Who to a friend his faults can freely show,
And gladly praise the merit of a foe?

1. Tom D'Urfey (1653–1723); poet and dramatist.
2. See p. 4, n. 2.
3. St. Paul's Cathedral was once a fashionable resort for idlers.

Blest with a taste exact, yet unconfin'd;
A knowledge both of books and human kind;
Gen'rous converse; a soul exempt from pride;
And love to praise, with reason on his side?

    Such once were Critics; such the happy few,
Athens and Rome in better ages knew.
The mighty Stagirite first left the shore,
Spread all his sails, and durst the deeps explore;
He steer'd securely, and discover'd far,
Led by the light of the Maeonian star.[1]
Poets, a race long unconfin'd, and free,
Still fond and proud of savage liberty,
Receiv'd his laws; and stood convinc'd 'twas fit,
Who conquer'd Nature, should preside o'er Wit.

    Horace still charms with graceful negligence,
And without method talks us into sense,
Will, like a friend, familiarly convey
The truest notions in the easiest way.
He who, supreme in judgment, as in wit,
Might boldly censure, as he boldly writ,
Yet judg'd with coolness, tho' he sung with fire;
His Precepts teach but what his works inspire.
Our Critics take a contrary extreme,
They judge with fury, but they write with phlegm:
Nor suffers Horace more in wrong Translations
By Wits, than Critics in as wrong Quotations.

    .   .   .   .   .

    Thus long succeeding Critics justly reign'd,
Licence repress'd, and useful laws ordain'd.
Learning and Rome alike in empire grew;
And Arts still follow'd where her Eagles flew;
From the same foes, at last, both felt their doom,
And the same age saw Learning fall, and Rome.

           1. Homer.

With Tyranny then Superstition join'd,
As that the body, this enslav'd the mind;
Much was believ'd, but little understood,
And to be dull was constru'd to be good;
A second deluge Learning thus o'er-run,
And the Monks finish'd what the Goths begun.

At length Erasmus, that great injur'd name,
(The glory of the Priesthood, and the shame!)
Stem'd the wild torrent of a barb'rous age,
And drove those holy Vandals off the stage.

But see! each Muse, in LEO's golden days,
Starts from her trance, and trims her wither'd bays,
Rome's ancient Genius, o'er its ruins spread,
Shakes off the dust, and rears his rev'rend head.
Then Sculpture and her sister-arts revive;
Stones leap'd to form, and rocks began to live;
With sweeter notes each rising Temple rung:
A Raphael painted, and a Vida sung:[1]
Immortal Vida: on whose honour'd brow
The Poet's bays and Critic's ivy grow;
Cremona now shall ever boast thy name,
As next in place to Mantua,[2] next in fame!

But soon by impious arms from Latium chas'd,
Their ancient bounds the banish'd Muses pass'd;
Thence Arts o'er all the northern world advance,
But Critic-learning flourish'd most in France:
The rules a nation, born to serve, obeys;
And Boileau still in right of Horace sways.[3]
But we, brave Britons, foreign laws despis'd,
And kept unconquer'd, and uncivilis'd;

1. Vida, an excellent Latin poet, who writ an Art of Poetry in verse.
He flourished in the time of Leo X. *P.*
2. See p. 17, n. 1.
3. Nicolas Boileau (1636–1711); French critic and poet.

Fierce for the liberties of wit, and bold,
We still defy'd the Romans, as of old.
Yet some there were, among the sounder few
Of those who less presum'd, and better knew,
Who durst assert the juster ancient cause,
And here restor'd Wit's fundamental laws.
Such was the Muse,[1] whose rules and practice tell,
'Nature's chief Masterpiece is writing well.'
Such was Roscommon,[2] not more learn'd than good,
With manners gen'rous as his noble blood;
To him the wit of Greece and Rome was known,
And ev'ry author's merit, but his own.
Such late was Walsh[3] – the Muse's judge and friend,
Who justly knew to blame or to commend;
To failings mild, but zealous for desert;
The clearest head, and the sincerest heart.
This humble praise, lamented shade! receive,
This praise at least a grateful Muse may give:
The Muse, whose early voice you taught to sing,
Prescrib'd her heights, and prun'd her tender wing,
(Her guide now lost) no more attempts to rise,
But in low numbers short excursions tries:
Content, if hence th' unlearn'd their wants may view,
The learn'd reflect on what before they knew:
Careless of censure, nor too fond of fame;
Still pleas'd to praise, yet not afraid to blame;
Averse alike to flatter, or offend;
Not free from faults, nor yet too vain to mend.

1. The Duke of Buckingham (1648–1721); politician, poetaster, and friend of Pope's.
2. Wentworth Dillon, Earl of Roscommon (1633?–85); poet and critic.
3. See p. 10, n. 1.

WINDSOR-FOREST

FIELD-SPORTS

YE vig'rous swains! while youth ferments your blood,
And purer spirits swell the sprightly flood,
Now range the hills, the gameful woods beset,
Wind the shrill horn, or spread the waving net.
When milder autumn summer's heat succeeds,
And in the new-shorn field the partridge feeds,
Before his lord the ready spaniel bounds,
Panting with hope, he tries the furrow'd grounds;
But when the tainted gales the game betray,
Couch'd close he lies, and meditates the prey:
Secúre they trust th' unfaithful field beset,
Till hov'ring o'er 'em sweeps the swelling net.
Thus (if small things we may with great compare)
When Albion sends her eager sons to war,
Some thoughtless Town, with ease and plenty blest,
Near, and more near, the closing lines invest;
Sudden they seize th' amaz'd, defenceless prize,
And high in air Britannia's standard flies.
    See! from the brake the whirring pheasant springs,
And mounts exulting on triumphant wings:
Short is his joy; he feels the fiery wound,
Flutters in blood, and panting beats the ground.
Ah! what avail his glossy, varying dyes,
His purple crest, and scarlet-circled eyes,
The vivid green his shining plumes unfold,
His painted wings, and breast that flames with gold?
    Nor yet, when moist Arcturus clouds the sky,
The woods and fields their pleasing toils deny.

To plains with well-breath'd beagles we repair,
And trace the mazes of the circling hare:
(Beasts, urg'd by us, their fellow-beasts pursue,
And learn of man each other to undo.)
With slaught'ring guns th' unwearied fowler roves,
When frosts have whiten'd all the naked groves;
Where doves in flocks the leafless trees o'ershade,
And lonely woodcocks haunt the wat'ry glade.
He lifts the tube, and levels with his eye;
Straight a short thunder breaks the frozen sky:
Oft, as in airy rings they skim the heath,
The clam'rous lapwings feel the leaden death:
Oft, as the mounting larks their notes prepare,
They fall, and leave their little lives in air.

In genial spring, beneath the quiv'ring shade,
Where cooling vapours breathe along the mead,
The patient fisher takes his silent stand,
Intent, his angle trembling in his hand:
With looks unmov'd, he hopes the scaly breed,
And eyes the dancing cork, the bending reed.
Our plenteous streams a various race supply,
The bright-ey'd perch with fins of Tyrian dye,
The silver eel, in shining volumes roll'd,
The yellow carp, in scales bedrop'd with gold,
Swift trouts, diversify'd with crimson stains,
And pykes, the tyrants of the wat'ry plains.

Now Cancer glows with Phoebus' fiery car:
The youth rush eager to the sylvan war,
Swarm o'er the lawns, the forest walks surround,
Rouze the fleet hart, and cheer the opening hound.
Th' impatient courser pants in ev'ry vein,
And pawing, seems to beat the distant plain:
Hills, vales, and floods appear already cross'd,
And ere he starts, a thousand steps are lost.

See the bold youth strain up the threat'ning steep,
Rush through the thickets, down the valleys sweep,
Hang o'er their coursers' heads with eager speed,
And earth rolls back beneath the flying steed.

THE RAPE OF THE LOCK

AN HEROI-COMICAL POEM

TO MRS ARABELLA FERMOR[1]

MADAM,

IT will be in vain to deny that I have some regard for this
piece, since I dedicate it to You. Yet you may bear me witness,
it was intended only to divert a few young Ladies, who have
good sense and good humour enough to laugh not only at their
sex's little unguarded follies, but at their own. But as it was
communicated with the air of a Secret, it soon found its way
into the world. An imperfect copy having been offer'd to a
Bookseller, you had the good-nature for my sake to consent to
the publication of one more correct: This I was forc'd to,
before I had executed half my design, for the Machinery was
entirely wanting to complete it.

The Machinery, Madam, is a term invented by the Critics,
to signify that part which the Deities, Angels, or Demons, are
made to act in a Poem: For the ancient Poets are in one respect
like many modern Ladies: let an action be never so trivial in
itself, they always make it appear of the utmost importance.
These Machines I determin'd to raise on a very new and odd
foundation, the Rosicrucian doctrine of Spirits.

I know how disagreeable it is to make use of hard words
before a Lady; but 'tis so much the concern of a Poet to have
his works understood, and particularly by your Sex, that you
must give me leave to explain two or three difficult terms.

The Rosicrucians are a people I must bring you acquainted
with. The best account I know of them is in a French book
call'd *Le Comte de Gabalis*, which both in its title and size is so
like a Novel, that many of the Fair Sex have read it for one by
mistake. According, to these Gentlemen, the four Elements are
inhabited by Spirits which they call Sylphs, Gnomes, Nymphs,

1. Lord Petre, the *Baron* of the poem, cut off a lock of Miss Arabella
    Fermor's hair, which occasioned a quarrel between their two
    families. Pope, at the instigation of a mutual friend, John Caryll,
    wrote this poem to heal the breach.

and Salamanders. The Gnomes or Demons of Earth delight in mischief; but the Sylphs, whose habitation is in the Air, are the best condition'd creatures imaginable. For they say, any mortals may enjoy the most intimate familiarities with these gentle Spirits, upon a condition very easy to all true Adepts, an inviolate preservation of Chastity.

As to the following Cantos, all the passages of them are as fabulous, as the Vision at the beginning, or the Transformation at the end; (except the loss of your Hair, which I always mention with reverence.) The Human persons are as fictitious as the Airy ones; and the character of Belinda, as it is now manag'd, resembles you in nothing but in Beauty.

If this Poem had as many Graces as there are in your Person, or in your Mind, yet I could never hope it should pass through the world half so Uncensur'd as You have done. But let its fortune be what it will, mine is happy enough, to have given me this occasion of assuring you that I am, with the truest esteem,

> MADAM,
>> *Your most obedient, humble servant,*
>>> A. POPE.

CANTO I

WHAT dire offence from am'rous causes springs,
What mighty contests rise from trivial things,
I sing – This verse to CARYL, Muse! is due:
This, ev'n Belinda may vouchsafe to view:
Slight is the subject, but not so the praise,
If She inspire, and He approve my lays.

Say what strange motive, Goddess! could compel
A well-bred Lord t' assault a gentle Belle?
O say what stranger cause, yet unexplor'd,
Could make a gentle Belle reject a Lord?
In tasks so bold, can little men engage,
And in soft bosoms, dwells such mighty Rage?

Sol, through white curtains shot a tim'rous ray,
And ope'd those eyes that must eclipse the day:
Now lap-dogs give themselves the rousing shake,
And sleepless lovers, just at twelve, awake:
Thrice rung the bell, the slipper knock'd the ground,
And the press'd watch return'd a silver sound.
Belinda still her downy pillow prest,
Her guardian SYLPH prolong'd the balmy rest:
'Twas He had summon'd to her silent bed
The morning-dream that hover'd o'er her head,
A Youth more glitt'ring than a Birth-night Beau,
(That ev'n in slumber caus'd her cheek to glow)
Seem'd to her ear his winning lips to lay,
And thus in whispers said, or seem'd to say.

'Fairest of mortals, thou distinguish'd care
Of thousand bright Inhabitants of Air!
If e'er one Vision touch thy infant thought,
Of all the Nurse and all the Priest have taught;
Of airy Elves by moonlight shadows seen,
The silver token, and the circled green,
Or virgins visited by Angel-pow'rs
With golden crowns and wreaths of heav'nly flow'rs;
Hear and believe! thy own importance know,
Nor bound thy narrow views to things below.
Some secret truths, from learned pride conceal'd,
To Maids alone and Children are reveal'd:
What tho' no credit doubting Wits may give?
The Fair and Innocent shall still believe.
Know then, unnumber'd Spirits round thee fly,
The light Militia of the lower sky:
These, tho' unseen, are ever on the wing,
Hang o'er the Box, and hover round the Ring.[1]

1. A fashionable parade in Hyde Park.

Think what an equipage thou hast in Air,
And view with scorn two Pages and a Chair.
As now your own, our beings were of old,
And once inclos'd in Woman's beauteous mould;
Thence, by a soft transition, we repair
From earthly Vehicles to these of air.
Think not, when Woman's transient breath is fled,
That all her vanities at once are dead;
Succeeding vanities she still regards,
And tho' she plays no more, o'erlooks the cards.
Her joy in gilded Chariots, when alive,
And love of Ombre, after death survive.
For when the Fair in all their pride expire,
To their first Elements their Souls retire:
The Sprites of fiery Termagants in Flame
Mount up, and take a Salamander's name.
Soft yielding minds to Water glide away,
And sip, with Nymphs, their elemental Tea.
The graver Prude sinks downward to a Gnome,
In search of mischief still on Earth to roam.
The light coquettes in Sylphs aloft repair,
And sport and flutter in the fields of air.

'Know farther yet; whoever fair and chaste
Rejects mankind, is by some Sylph embrac'd:
For Spirits, freed from mortal laws, with ease
Assume what sexes and what shapes they please.
What guards the purity of melting Maids,
In courtly balls, and midnight masquerades,
Safe from the treach'rous friend, the daring spark,
The glance by day, the whisper in the dark,
When kind occasion prompts their warm desires,
When music softens, and when dancing fires?
'Tis but their Sylph, the wise Celestials know,
Though Honour is the word with Men below.

'Some nymphs there are, too conscious of their face,
For life predestin'd to the Gnomes embrace.
These swell their prospects and exalt their pride,
When offers are disdain'd, and love deny'd;
Then gay Ideas crowd the vacant brain,
While Peers, and Dukes, and all their sweeping
    train,
And Garters, Stars, and Coronets appear,
And in soft sounds, 'YOUR GRACE' salutes their ear.
'Tis these that early taint the female soul,
Instruct the eyes of young Coquettes to roll,
Teach Infant-cheeks a bidden blush to know,
And little hearts to flutter at a Beau.

'Oft, when the world imagine women stray,
The Sylphs through mystic mazes guide their way,
Through all the giddy circle they pursue,
And old impertinence expell by new.
What tender maid but must a victim fall
To one man's treat, but for another's ball?
When Florio speaks, what virgin could withstand,
If gentle Damon did not squeeze her hand?
With varying vanities, from ev'ry part,
They shift the moving Toyshop of their heart;
Where wigs with wigs, with sword-knots sword-
    knots strive,
Beaux banish beaux, and coaches coaches drive.
This erring mortals Levity may call,
Oh, blind to truth! the Sylphs contrive it all.

'Of these am I, who thy protection claim,
A watchful sprite, and Ariel is my name.
Late, as I rang'd the crystal wilds of air,
In the clear Mirror of thy ruling Star
I saw, alas! some dread event impend,
Ere to the main this morning sun descend,

But heav'n reveals not what, or how, or where:
Warn'd by the Sylph, oh pious maid, beware!
This to disclose is all thy guardian can:
Beware of all, but most beware of Man!'

    He said; when Shock, who thought she slept too long,
Leap'd up, and wak'd his mistress with his tongue.
'Twas then, Belinda, if report say true,
Thy eyes first open'd on a Billet-doux;
Wounds, Charms, and Ardours, were no sooner read,
But all the Vision vanish'd from thy head.

    And now, unveil'd, the Toilet stands display'd,
Each silver Vase in mystic order laid.
First, rob'd in white, the Nymph intent adores,
With head uncover'd, the Cosmetic pow'rs.
A heav'nly Image in the glass appears,
To that she bends, to that her eyes she rears;
Th' inferior Priestess, at her altar's side,
Trembling begins the sacred rites of Pride.
Unnumber'd treasures ope at once, and here
The various off'rings of the world appear;
From each she nicely culls with curious toil,
And decks the Goddess with the glitt'ring spoil.
This casket India's glowing gems unlocks,
And all Arabia breathes from yonder box.
The Tortoise here and Elephant unite,
Transform'd to combs, the speckled, and the white.
Here files of pins extend their shining rows,
Puffs, Powders, Patches, Bibles, Billet-doux.
Now awful Beauty puts on all its arms;
The fair each moment rises in her charms,
Repairs her smiles, awakens ev'ry grace,
And calls forth all the wonders of her face;
Sees by degrees a purer blush arise,
And keener lightnings quicken in her eyes.

The busy Sylphs surround their darling care,
These set the head, and those divide the hair,
Some fold the sleeve, whilst others plait the gown;
And Betty's prais'd for labours not her own.

NOT with more glories, in th' ethereal plain,
The Sun first rises o'er the purpled main,
Than, issuing forth, the rival of his beams
Launch'd on the bosom of the silver Thames.
Fair Nymphs, and well-drest Youths around her shone,
But ev'ry eye was fix'd on her alone.
On her white breast a sparkling Cross she wore,
Which Jews might kiss, and Infidels adore.
Her lively looks a sprightly mind disclose,
Quick as her eyes, and as unfix'd as those:
Favours to none, to all she smiles extends;
Oft she rejects, but never once offends.
Bright as the sun, her eyes the gazers strike,
And, like the sun, they shine on all alike.
Yet graceful ease, and sweetness void of pride,
Might hide her faults, if Belles had faults to hide:
If to her share some female errors fall,
Look on her face, and you'll forget 'em all.

This Nymph, to the destruction of mankind,
Nourish'd two Locks, which graceful hung behind
In equal curls, and well conspir'd to deck
With shining ringlets the smooth iv'ry neck.
Love in these labyrinths his slaves detains,
And mighty hearts are held in slender chains.
With hairy springes we the birds betray,
Slight lines of hair surprise the finny prey,

Fair tresses man's imperial race insnare,
And beauty draws us with a single hair.

Th' advent'rous Baron the bright locks admir'd;
He saw, he wish'd, and to the prize aspir'd.
Resolv'd to win, he meditates the way,
By force to ravish, or by fraud betray;
For when success a Lover's toil attends,
Few ask, if fraud or force attain'd his ends.

For this, ere Phoebus rose, he had implor'd
Propitious Heav'n, and ev'ry pow'r ador'd,
But chiefly Love – to Love an Altar built,
Of twelve vast French Romances, neatly gilt.
There lay three garters, half a pair of gloves,
And all the trophies of his former loves;
With tender Billet-doux he lights the pyre,
And breathes three am'rous sighs to raise the fire.
Then prostrate falls, and begs with ardent eyes
Soon to obtain, and long possess the prize:
The pow'rs gave ear, and granted half his pray'r,
The rest, the winds dispers'd in empty air.

But now secure the painted vessel glides,
The sun-beams trembling on the floating tides:
While melting music steals upon the sky,
And soften'd sounds along the waters die;
Smooth flow the waves, the Zephyrs gently play,
Belinda smil'd, and all the world was gay.
All but the Sylph – with careful thoughts opprest,
Th' impending woe sat heavy on his breast.
He summons straight his Denizens of air;
The lucid squadrons round the sails repair;
Soft o'er the shrouds aërial whispers breathe,
That seem'd but Zephyrs to the train beneath.
Some to the sun their insect-wings unfold,
Waft on the breeze, or sink in clouds of gold:

Transparent forms, too fine for mortal sight,
Their fluid bodies half dissolv'd in light.
Loose to the wind their airy garments flew,
Thin glitt'ring textures of the filmy dew,
Dipt in the richest tincture of the skies,
Where light disports in ever-mingling dyes;
While ev'ry beam new transient colours flings,
Colours that change whene'er they wave their wings.
Amid the circle, on the gilded mast,
Superior by the head, was Ariel plac'd;
His purple pinions op'ning to the sun,
He rais'd his azure wand, and thus begun.

  'Ye Sylphs and Sylphids, to your chief give ear,
Fays, Fairies, Genii, Elves, and Demons hear!
Ye know the spheres and various tasks assign'd
By laws eternal to th' aerial kind.
Some in the fields of purest Ether play,
And bask and whiten in the blaze of day.
Some guide the course of wand'ring orbs on high,
Or roll the planets through the boundless sky.
Some less refin'd, beneath the moon's pale light
Pursue the stars that shoot athwart the night,
Or suck the mists in grosser air below,
Or dip their pinions in the painted bow,
Or brew fierce tempests on the wintry main,
Or o'er the glebe distil the kindly rain.
Others on earth o'er human race preside,
Watch all their ways, and all their actions guide:
Of these the chief the care of Nations own,
And guard with Arms divine the British Throne.

  'Our humbler province is to tend the Fair,
Not a less pleasing, tho' less glorious care;
To save the powder from too rude a gale,
Nor let th' imprison'd essences exhale;

To draw fresh colours from the vernal flow'rs;
To steal from rainbows, e'er they drop in show'rs
A brighter wash; to curl their waving hairs,
Assist their blushes, and inspire their airs;
Nay oft, in dreams, invention we bestow,
To change a Flounce, or add a Furbelow.

'This day, black Omens threat the brightest Fair
That e'er deserv'd a watchful spirit's care;
Some dire disaster, or by force, or slight;
But what, or where, the fates have wrapt in night.
Whether the nymph shall break Diana's law,
Or some frail China jar receive a flaw;
Or stain her honour, or her new brocade;
Forget her pray'rs, or miss a masquerade;
Or lose her heart, or necklace, at a ball;
Or whether Heav'n has doom'd that Shock must fall.
Haste then, ye spirits! to your charge repair:
The flutt'ring fan be Zephyretta's care;
The drops to thee, Brillante, we consign;
And, Momentilla, let the watch be thine;
Do thou, Crispissa, tend her fav'rite Lock;
Ariel himself shall be the guard of Shock.

'To fifty chosen Sylphs, of special note,
We trust th' important charge, the Petticoat:
Oft have we known that seven-fold fence to fail,
Tho' stiff with hoops, and arm'd with ribs of whale;
Form a strong line about the silver bound,
And guard the wide circumference around.

'Whatever spirit, careless of his charge,
His post neglects, or leaves the fair at large,
Shall feel sharp vengeance soon o'ertake his sins,
Be stop'd in vials, or transfix'd with pins;
Or plung'd in lakes of bitter washes lie,
Or wedg'd whole ages in a bodkin's eye:

Gums and Pomatums shall his flight restrain,
While, clog'd, he beats his silken wings in vain;
Or Alum styptics with contracting pow'r
Shrink his thin essence like a rivel'd flow'r:
Or, as Ixion fix'd, the wretch shall feel
The giddy motion of the whirling Mill,
In fumes of burning Chocolate shall glow,
And tremble at the sea that froths below!'

He spoke; the spirits from the sails descend;
Some, orb in orb, around the nymph extend;
Some thrid the mazy ringlets of her hair;
Some hang upon the pendants of her ear;
With beating hearts the dire event they wait,
Anxious, and trembling for the birth of Fate.

CANTO III

CLOSE by those meads, for ever crown'd with flow'rs,
Where Thames with pride surveys his rising tow'rs,
There stands a structure of majestic frame,
Which from the neighb'ring Hampton takes its name.
Here Britain's statesmen oft the fall foredoom
Of foreign Tyrants, and of Nymphs at home;
Here thou, great ANNA! whom three realms obey,
Dost sometimes counsel take – and sometimes Tea.

Hither the Heroes and the Nymphs resort,
To taste awhile the pleasures of a Court;
In various talk th' instructive hours they past,
Who gave the ball, or paid the visit last;
One speaks the glory of the British Queen,
And one describes a charming Indian screen;
A third interprets motions, looks, and eyes;
At ev'ry word a reputation dies.

Snuff, or the fan, supply each pause of chat,
With singing, laughing, ogling, *and all that*.

Mean while, declining from the noon of day,
The sun obliquely shoots his burning ray;
The hungry Judges soon the sentence sign,
And wretches hang that Jury-men may dine;
The merchant from th' Exchange returns in peace,
And the long labours of the Toilet cease.
Belinda now, whom thirst of fame invites,
Burns to encounter two advent'rous Knights,
At Ombre[1] singly to decide their doom;
And swells her breast with conquests yet to come.
Straight the three bands prepare in arms to join,
Each band the number of the sacred Nine.
Soon as she spreads her hand, th' aërial guard
Descend, and sit on each important card:
First Ariel perch'd upon a Matadore,
Then each according to the rank they bore;
For Sylphs, yet mindful of their ancient race,
Are, as when women, wond'rous fond of place.

Behold, four Kings in majesty rever'd,
With hoary whiskers and a forky beard;
And four fair Queens whose hands sustain a flow'r,
Th' expressive emblem of their softer pow'r;
Four Knaves in garbs succinct, a trusty band,
Caps on their heads, and halberts in their hand;
And particolour'd troops, a shining train,
Draw forth to combat on the velvet plain.

The skilful Nymph reviews her force with care:
'Let Spades be trumps!' she said, and trumps they
    were.

Now move to war her sable Matadores,
In show like leaders of the swarthy Moors.

1. A card game played by three players with a pack of forty cards.

Spadillio[1] first, unconquerable Lord!
Led off two captive trumps, and swept the board.
As many more Manillio[2] forc'd to yield,
And march'd a victor from the verdant field.
Him Basto[3] follow'd, but his fate more hard
Gain'd but one trump and one Plebeian card.
With his broad sabre next, a chief in years,
The hoary Majesty of Spades appears,
Puts forth one manly leg, to sight reveal'd,
The rest, his many-colour'd robe conceal'd.
The rebel Knave, who dares his prince engage,
Proves the just victim of his royal rage.
Ev'n mighty Pam[4], that Kings and Queens o'er-threw
And mow'd down armies in the fights of Loo,
Sad chance of war! now destitute of aid,
Falls undistinguish'd by the victor Spade!

Thus far both armies to Belinda yield;
Now to the Baron fate inclines the field.
His warlike Amazon her host invades,
Th' imperial consort of the crown of Spades.
The Club's black Tyrant first her victim dy'd,
Spite of his haughty mien, and barb'rous pride:
What boots the regal circle on his head,
His giant limbs, in state unwieldy spread;
That long behind he trails his pompous robe,
And, of all monarchs, only grasps the globe?

The Baron now his Diamonds pours apace;
Th' embroider'd King who shows but half his face,
And his refulgent Queen, with pow'rs combin'd,
Of broken troops an easy conquest find.
Clubs, Diamonds, Hearts, in wild disorder seen,
With throngs promiscuous strow the level green.

1. Ace of Spades.   2. Two of Spades.
3. Ace of Clubs.   4. Knave of Clubs.

Thus when dispers'd a routed army runs,
Of Asia's troops, and Afric's sable sons,
With like confusion different nations fly,
Of various habit and of various dye;
The pierc'd battalions disunited fall,
In heaps on heaps; one fate o'erwhelms them all.

    The Knave of Diamonds tries his wily arts,
And wins (oh shameful chance!) the Queen of Hearts.
At this, the blood the virgin's cheek forsook,
A livid paleness spreads o'er all her look;
She sees, and trembles at th' approaching ill,
Just in the jaws of ruin, and Codille[1].
And now, (as oft in some distemper'd State)
On one nice Trick depends the gen'ral fate:
An Ace of Hearts steps forth: the King unseen
Lurk'd in her hand, and mourn'd his captive Queen:
He springs to vengeance with an eager pace,
And falls like thunder on the prostrate Ace.
The nymph, exulting, fills with shouts the sky;
The walls, the woods, and long canals reply.

    O thoughtless mortals! ever blind to fate,
Too soon dejected, and too soon elate.
Sudden these honours shall be snatch'd away,
And curs'd for ever this victorious day.

    For lo! the board with cups and spoons is crown'd,
The berries crackle, and the mill turns round;
On shining altars of Japan they raise
The silver lamp; the fiery spirits blaze:
From silver spouts the grateful liquors glide,
While China's earth receives the smoking tide:
At once they gratify their sense and taste,
And frequent cups prolong the rich repast.

1. Loss of the game.

Straight hover round the Fair her airy band;
Some, as she sipp'd, the fuming liquor fann'd,
Some o'er her lap their careful plumes display'd,
Trembling, and conscious of the rich brocade.
Coffee (which makes the politician wise,
And see through all things with his half-shut eyes)
Sent up in vapours to the Baron's brain
New stratagems, the radiant Lock to gain.
Ah cease, rash youth! desist ere 'tis too late,
Fear the just Gods, and think of Scylla's Fate!
Chang'd to a bird, and sent to flit in air,
She dearly pays for Nisus' injur'd hair!

But when to mischief mortals bend their will,
How soon they find fit instruments of ill?
Just then, Clarissa drew with tempting grace
A two-edg'd weapon from her shining case:
So Ladies in Romance assist their Knight,
Present the spear, and arm him for the fight.
He takes the gift with rev'rence, and extends
The little engine on his fingers' ends;
This just behind Belinda's neck he spread,
As o'er the fragrant steams she bends her head.
Swift to the Lock a thousand Sprites repair,
A thousand wings, by turns, blow back the hair;
And thrice they twitch'd the diamond in her ear;
Thrice she look'd back, and thrice the foe drew near.
Just in that instant, anxious Ariel sought
The close recesses of the Virgin's thought;
As on the nosegay in her breast reclin'd,
He watch'd th' ideas rising in her mind,
Sudden he view'd, in spite of all her art,
An earthly Lover lurking at her heart.
Amaz'd, confus'd, he found his pow'r expir'd,
Resign'd to fate, and with a sigh retir'd.

The Peer now spreads the glitt'ring Forfex wide,
T' inclose the Lock; now joins it, to divide.
Ev'n then, before the fatal engine clos'd,
A wretched Sylph too fondly interpos'd;
Fate urg'd the sheers, and cut the Sylph in twain,
(But airy substance soon unites again)
The meeting points the sacred hair dissever
From the fair head, for ever, and for ever!

Then flash'd the living lightning from her eyes,
And screams of horror rend th' affrighted skies.
Not louder shrieks to pitying heav'n are cast,
When husbands, or when lap-dogs breathe their last;
Or when rich China vessels, fall'n from high,
In glitt'ring dust and painted fragments lie!

'Let wreaths of triumph now my temples twine,
(The Victor cry'd) the glorious Prize is mine!
While fish in streams, or birds delight in air,
Or in a coach-and-six the British Fair,
As long as Atalantis[1] shall be read,
Or the small pillow grace a Lady's bed,
While visits shall be paid on solemn days,
When num'rous wax-lights in bright order blaze,
While nymphs take treats, or assignations give,
So long my honour, name, and praise shall live!'

What Time would spare, from Steel receives its
        date,
And monuments, like men, submit to fate!
Steel could the labour of the Gods destroy,
And strike to dust th' imperial tow'rs of Troy;
Steel could the works of mortal pride confound,
And hew triumphal arches to the ground.
What wonder then, fair nymph! thy hairs should feel
The conqu'ring force of unresisted Steel?

1. A scandalous romance by Mrs Manley (1663-1724).

CANTO IV

But anxious cares the pensive nymph oppress'd,
And secret passions labour'd in her breast.
Not youthful kings in battle seiz'd alive,
Not scornful virgins who their charms survive,
Not ardent lovers robb'd of all their bliss,
Not ancient ladies when refus'd a kiss,
Not tyrants fierce that unrepenting die,
Not Cynthia when her manteau's pinn'd awry,
E'er felt such rage, resentment, and despair,
As thou, sad Virgin! for thy ravish'd Hair.

For, that sad moment, when the Sylphs withdrew,
And Ariel weeping from Belinda flew,
Umbriel, a dusky, melancholy sprite,
As ever sully'd the fair face of light,
Down to the central earth, his proper scene,
Repair'd to search the gloomy Cave of Spleen.

Swift on his sooty pinions flits the Gnome,
And in a vapour reach'd the dismal dome.
No cheerful breeze this sullen region knows,
The dreaded East is all the wind that blows.
Here in a grotto, shelter'd close from air,
And screen'd in shades from day's detested glare,
She sighs for ever on her pensive bed,
Pain at her side, and Megrim at her head.

Two handmaids wait the throne: alike in place,
But diff'ring far in figure and in face.
Here stood Ill-nature like an ancient maid,
Her wrinkled form in black and white array'd!
With store of pray'rs, for mornings, nights, and noons
Her hand is fill'd; her bosom with lampoons.

There Affectation, with a sickly mien,
Shows in her cheek the roses of eighteen,

Practis'd to lisp, and hang the head aside,
Faints into airs, and languishes with pride,
On the rich quilt sinks with becoming woe,
Wrapt in a gown, for sickness, and for show.
The fair-ones feel such maladies as these,
When each new night-dress gives a new disease.

A constant Vapour o'er the palace flies,
Strange phantoms rising as the mists arise;
Dreadful, as hermits dreams in haunted shades,
Or bright, as visions of expiring maids.
Now glaring fiends, and snakes on rolling spires,
Pale spectres, gaping tombs, and purple fires:
Now lakes of liquid gold, Elysian scenes,
And crystal domes, and Angels in machines.

Unnumber'd throngs, on ev'ry side are seen,
Of bodies chang'd to various forms by Spleen.
Here living Tea-pots stand, one arm held out,
One bent; the handle this, and that the spout:
A pipkin there, like Homer's Tripod walks;
Here sighs a Jar, and there a Goose-pye talks;
Men prove with child, as pow'rful fancy works,
And maids turn'd bottles, call aloud for corks.

Safe past the Gnome through this fantastic band,
A branch of healing Spleenwort in his hand.
Then thus address'd the pow'r – 'Hail, wayward Queen!
Who rule the sex to fifty from fifteen:
Parent of vapours and of female wit,
Who give th' hysteric, or poetic fit,
On various tempers act by various ways,
Make some take physic, others scribble plays;
Who cause the proud their visits to delay,
And send the godly in a pet to pray;
A nymph there is, that all thy pow'r disdains,
And thousands more in equal mirth maintains.

But oh! if e'er thy Gnome could spoil a grace,
Or raise a pimple on a beauteous face,
Like Citron-waters matrons cheeks inflame,
Or change complexions at a losing game;
If e'er with airy horns I planted heads,
Or rumpled petticoats, or tumbled beds,
Or caus'd suspicion when no soul was rude,
Or discompos'd the head-dress of a Prude,
Or e'er to costive lap dog gave disease,
Which not the tears of brightest eyes could ease:
Hear me, and touch Belinda with chagrin,
That single act gives half the world the spleen.'

 The Goddess with a discontented air
Seems to reject him, tho' she grants his pray'r.
A wond'rous Bag with both her hands she binds,
Like that where once Ulysses held the winds;
There she collects the force of female lungs,
Sighs, sobs, and passions, and the war of tongues.
A Vial next she fills with fainting fears,
Soft sorrows, melting griefs, and flowing tears.
The Gnome rejoicing bears her gifts away,
Spreads his black wings, and slowly mounts to day.

 Sunk in Thalestris' arms the nymph he found,
Her eyes dejected, and her hair unbound.
Full o'er their heads the swelling bag he rent,
And all the Furies issu'd at the vent.
Belinda burns with more than mortal ire,
And fierce Thalestris fans the rising fire.
'O wretched maid!' she spread her hands, and cry'd,
(While Hampton's echoes 'Wretched maid!' reply'd)
'Was it for this you took such constant care
The bodkin, comb, and essence to prepare?
For this your locks in paper durance bound?
For this with tort'ring irons wreath'd around?

For this with fillets strain'd your tender head?
And bravely bore the double loads of lead?
Gods! shall the ravisher display your hair,
While the Fops envy, and the Ladies stare?
Honour forbid! at whose unrival'd shrine
Ease, pleasure, virtue, all our sex resign.
Methinks already I your tears survey,
Already hear the horrid things they say,
Already see you a degraded toast,
And all your honour in a whisper lost!
How shall I, then, your helpless fame defend?
'Twill then be infamy to seem your friend!
And shall this prize, th' inestimable prize,
Expos'd through crystal to the gazing eyes,
And heighten'd by the diamond's circling rays,
On that rapacious hand for ever blaze?
Sooner shall grass in Hyde-park Circus grow,
And wits take lodgings in the sound of Bow;
Sooner let earth, air, sea, to Chaos fall,
Men, monkeys, lap-dogs, parrots, perish all!'

She said; then raging to Sir Plume repairs,
And bids her Beau demand the precious hairs:
(Sir Plume of amber snuff-box justly vain,
And the nice conduct of a clouded cane)
With earnest eyes, and round unthinking face,
He first the snuff-box open'd, then the case,
And thus broke out – 'My Lord, why, what the devil!
Z – ds! damn the Lock! 'fore Gad, you must be civil!
Plague on 't! 'tis past a jest – nay, prithee, pox!
Give her the hair' – he spoke, and rapp'd his box.

'It grieves me much' (reply'd the Peer again)
'Who speaks so well should ever speak in vain.
But by this Lock, this sacred Lock I swear,
(Which never more shall join its parted hair;

Which never more its honours shall renew,
Clip'd from the lovely head where late it grew)
That while my nostrils draw the vital air,
This hand, which won it, shall for ever wear.'
He spoke, and speaking, in proud triumph spread
The long-contended honours of her head.

But Umbriel, hateful Gnome! forbears not so,
He breaks the Vial whence the sorrows flow.
Then see! the nymph in beauteous grief appears,
Her eyes half-languishing, half-drown'd in tears;
On her heav'd bosom hung her drooping head,
Which, with a sigh, she rais'd; and thus she said.

'For ever curs'd be this detested day,
Which snatch'd my best, my fav'rite curl away!
Happy! ah ten times happy had I been,
If Hampton-Court these eyes had never seen!
Yet am not I the first mistaken maid,
By love of Courts to num'rous ills betray'd.
Oh had I rather un-admir'd remain'd
In some lone isle, or distant Northern land;
Where the gilt Chariot never marks the way,
Where none learn Ombre, none e'er taste Bohea!
There kept my charms conceal'd from mortal eye,
Like roses, that in deserts bloom and die.
What mov'd my mind with youthful Lords to roam?
O had I stay'd, and said my pray'rs at home!
'Twas this, the morning omens seem'd to tell:
Thrice from my trembling hand the patch-box fell;
The tott'ring China shook without a wind,
Nay Poll sat mute, and Shock was most unkind!
A Sylph too warn'd me of the threats of fate,
In mystic visions, now believ'd too late!
See the poor remnants of these slighted hairs!
My hands shall rend what ev'n thy rapine spares:

These in two sable ringlets taught to break,
Once gave new beauties to the snowy neck;
The sister-lock now sits uncouth, alone,
And in its fellow's fate foresees its own;
Uncurl'd it hangs, the fatal sheers demands,
And tempts, once more, thy sacrilegious hands.
Oh hadst thou, cruel! been content to seize
Hairs less in sight, or any hairs but these!'

CANTO V

SHE said: the pitying audience melt in tears,
But Fate and Jove had stopp'd the Baron's ears.
In vain Thalestris with reproach assails,
For who can move when fair Belinda fails?
Not half so fix'd the Trojan could remain,
While Anna begg'd and Dido rag'd in vain.
Then grave Clarissa graceful wav'd her fan;
Silence ensu'd, and thus the nymph began.

  'Say, why are Beauties prais'd and honour'd most,
The wise man's passion, and the vain man's toast?
Why deck'd with all that land and sea afford
Why Angels call'd, and Angel-like adored?
Why round our coaches crowd the white-glov'd Beaus.
Why bows the side-box from its inmost rows?
How vain are all these glories, all our pains,
Unless good sense preserve what beauty gains:
That men may say, when we the front-box grace,
Behold the first in virtue as in face!
Oh! if to dance all night, and dress all day,
Charm'd the small-pox, or chas'd old-age away;
Who would not scorn what housewife's cares produce,
Or who would learn one earthly thing of use?

To patch, nay ogle, might become a Saint,
Nor could it sure be such a sin to paint.
But since, alas! frail beauty must decay,
Curl'd or uncurl'd, since Locks will turn to grey;
Since painted, or not painted, all shall fade,
And she who scorns a man, must die a maid;
What then remains, but well our pow'r to use,
And keep good-humour still, whate'er we lose?
And trust me, dear! good-humour can prevail,
When airs, and flights, and screams, and scolding fail.
Beauties in vain their pretty eyes may roll;
Charms strike the sight, but merit wins the soul.'

So spoke the Dame, but no applause ensu'd;
Belinda frown'd, Thalestris call'd her Prude.
'To arms, to arms!' the fierce Virago cries,
And swift as lightning to the combat flies.
All side in parties, and begin th' attack;
Fans clap, silks russle, and tough whalebones crack;
Heroes' and Heroines' shouts confus'dly rise,
And base and treble voices strike the skies.
No common weapons in their hands are found,
Like Gods they fight, nor dread a mortal wound.

So when bold Homer makes the Gods engage,
And heav'nly breasts with human passions rage;
'Gainst Pallas, Mars; Latona, Hermes arms,
And all Olympus rings with loud alarms:
Jove's thunder roars, heav'n trembles all around,
Blue Neptune storms, the bellowing deeps re-
    sound:
Earth shakes her nodding tow'rs, the ground gives
    way,
And the pale ghosts start at the flash of day!

Triumphant Umbriel on a sconce's height
Clap'd his glad wings, and sat to view the fight:

Prop'd on their bodkin spears, the Sprites survey
The growing combat, or assist the fray.

While through the press enrag'd Thalestris flies,
And scatters death around from both her eyes,
A Beau and Witling perish'd in the throng,
One dy'd in metaphor, and one in song.
'O cruel nymph! a living death I bear,'
Cry'd Dapperwit, and sunk beside his chair.
A mournful glance Sir Fopling upwards cast,
'Those eyes are made so killing' – was his last.
Thus on Maeander's flow'ry margin lies
Th' expiring Swan, and as he sings he dies.

When bold Sir Plume had drawn Clarissa down,
Chloe stepp'd in, and kill'd him with a frown;
She smil'd to see the doughty hero slain,
But, at her smile, the Beau reviv'd again.

Now Jove suspends his golden scales in air,
Weighs the Men's wits against the Lady's hair;
The doubtful beam long nods from side to side;
At length the wits mount up, the hairs subside.

See fierce Belinda on the Baron flies,
With more than usual lightning in her eyes:
Nor fear'd the chief th' unequal fight to try,
Who sought no more than on his foe to die.
But this bold Lord, with manly strength endu'd,
She with one finger and a thumb subdu'd:
Just where the breath of life his nostrils drew,
A charge of snuff the wily virgin threw;
The Gnomes direct, to ev'ry atom just,
The pungent grains of titillating dust.
Sudden, with starting tears each eye o'erflows,
And the high dome re-echoes to his nose.

'Now meet thy fate!' incens'd Belinda cry'd,
And drew a deadly bodkin from her side,

(The same, his ancient personage to deck,
Her great great grandsire wore about his neck,
In three seal-rings; which after, melted down,
Form'd a vast buckle for his widow's gown:
Her infant grandame's whistle next it grew,
The bells she jingled, and the whistle blew;
Then in a bodkin grac'd her mother's hairs,
Which long she wore, and now Belinda wears.)
    'Boast not my fall,' (he cry'd) 'insulting foe!
Thou by some other shalt be laid as low.
Nor think, to die dejects my lofty mind;
All that I dread is leaving you behind!
Rather than so, ah let me still survive,
And burn in Cupid's flames – but burn alive.'
    'Restore the Lock!' she cries; and all around
'Restore the Lock!' the vaulted roofs rebound.
Not fierce Othello in so loud a strain
Roar'd for the handkerchief that caus'd his pain.
But see how oft ambitious aims are cross'd,
And chiefs contend 'till all the prize is lost!
The Lock, obtain'd with guilt, and kept with pain,
In ev'ry place is sought, but sought in vain:
With such a prize no mortal must be blest,
So Heav'n decrees! with Heav'n who can contest?
    Some thought it mounted to the Lunar sphere,
Since all things lost on earth are treasur'd there.
There Heroes' wits are kept in pond'rous vases,
And Beaux' in snuff-boxes and tweezer-cases.
There broken vows, and death-bed alms are found,
And lovers hearts with ends of ribband bound,
The courtier's promises, and sick man's pray'rs,
The smiles of harlots, and the tears of heirs,
Cages for gnats, and chains to yoak a flea,
Dry'd butterflies, and tomes of casuistry.

But trust the Muse – she saw it upward rise,
Tho' mark'd by none but quick, poetic eyes:
(So Rome's great founder to the heav'ns withdrew,
To Proculus alone confess'd in view)
A sudden Star, it shot through liquid air,
And drew behind a radiant trail of hair.
Not Berenice's Locks first rose so bright,
The heav'ns bespangling with dishevel'd light.
The Sylphs behold it kindling as it flies,
And pleas'd pursue its progress through the skies.

This the Beau monde shall from the Mall survey,
And hail with music its propitious ray;
This the bless'd Lover shall for Venus take,
And send up vows from Rosamonda's lake;[1]
This Partridge[2] soon shall view in cloudless skies,
When next he looks through Galileo's eyes;
And hence th' egregious wizard shall foredoom
The fate of Louis, and the fall of Rome.

Then cease, bright Nymph! to mourn thy ravish'd
hair,
Which adds new glory to the shining sphere!
Not all the tresses that fair head can boast,
Shall draw such envy as the Lock you lost.
For, after all the murders of your eye,
When, after millions slain, yourself shall die;
When those fair suns shall set, as set they must,
And all those tresses shall be laid in dust,
This Lock, the Muse shall consecrate to fame,
And 'midst the stars inscribe Belinda's name.

1. A pond once in St James's Park.
2. John Partridge was a ridiculous star-gazer, who in his Almanacks
every year, never fail'd to predict the downfall of the Pope, and the
King of France, then at war with the English. P.

THE TEMPLE OF FAME

WHILE thus I stood, intent to see and hear,
One came, methought, and whisper'd in my ear:
'What could thus high thy rash ambition raise?
Art thou, fond youth, a candidate for praise?'
  ' 'Tis true,' said I, 'not void of hopes I came,
For who so fond as youthful bards of Fame?
But few, alas! the casual blessing boast,
So hard to gain, so easy to be lost.
How vain that second life in others breath,
Th' estate which wits inherit after death!
Ease, health, and life, for this they must resign,
(Unsure the tenure, but how vast the fine!)
The great man's curse, without the gains, endure,
Be envied, wretched, and be flatter'd, poor;
All luckless wits their enemies profest,
And all successful, jealous friends at best.
Nor Fame I slight, nor for her favours call;
She comes unlook'd for, if she comes at all.
But if the purchase costs so dear a price,
As soothing Folly, or exalting Vice:
Oh! if the Muse must flatter lawless sway,
And follow still where fortune leads the way;
Or if no basis bear my rising name,
But the fall'n ruins of another's fame;
Then teach me, heav'n! to scorn the guilty bays,
Drive from my breast that wretched lust of praise;
Unblemish'd let me live, or die unknown;
Oh, grant an honest fame, or grant me none!'

ELOISA TO ABELARD

Abelard and Eloisa flourished in the twelfth century; they were two of the most distinguished persons of their age in learning and beauty, but for nothing more famous than for their unfortunate passion. After a long course of calamities, they retired each to a several Convent, and consecrated the remainder of their days to religion. It was many years after this separation, that a letter of Abelard's to a Friend, which contained the history of his misfortune, fell into the hands of Eloisa. This awakening all her tenderness, occasioned those celebrated letters (out of which the following is partly extracted) which give so lively a picture of the struggles of grace and nature, virtue and passion. P.

In these deep solitudes and awful cells,
Where heav'nly-pensive contemplation dwells,
And ever-musing melancholy reigns,
What means this tumult in a Vestal's veins?
Why rove my thoughts beyond this last retreat?
Why feels my heart its long-forgotten heat?
Yet, yet I love! – From Abelard it came,
And Eloisa yet must kiss the name.

Dear fatal name! rest ever unreveal'd,
Nor pass these lips in holy silence seal'd:
Hide it, my heart, within that close disguise,
Where, mix'd with God's, his lov'd Idea lies:
Oh write it not, my hand – the name appears
Already written – wash it out, my tears!
In vain lost Eloisa weeps and prays,
Her heart still dictates, and her hand obeys.

Relentless walls! whose darksome round contains
Repentant sighs, and voluntary pains:
Ye rugged rocks, which holy knees have worn;
Ye grots and caverns, shagg'd with horrid thorn!
Shrines! where their vigils pale-ey'd virgins keep,
And pitying saints, whose statues learn to weep!
Tho' cold like you, unmov'd and silent grown,
I have not yet forgot myself to stone.

All is not Heav'n's while Abelard has part,
Still rebel nature holds out half my heart;
Nor pray'rs nor fasts its stubborn pulse restrain,
Nor tears for ages taught to flow in vain.
　　Soon as thy letters trembling I unclose,
That well-known name awakens all my woes.
Oh name for ever sad! for ever dear!
Still breath'd in sighs, still usher'd with a tear.
I tremble too, where'er my own I find,
Some dire misfortune follows close behind.
Line after line my gushing eyes o'erflow,
Led through a sad variety of woe:
Now warm in love, now with'ring in my bloom,
Lost in a convent's solitary gloom!
There stern Religion quench'd th' unwilling flame,
There dy'd the best of passions, Love and Fame.
　　Yet write, oh write me all, that I may join
Griefs to thy griefs, and echo sighs to thine.
Nor foes nor fortune take this pow'r away;
And is my Abelard less kind than they?
Tears still are mine, and those I need not spare,
Love but demands what else were shed in pray'r;
No happier task these faded eyes pursue;
To read and weep is all they now can do.
　　Then share thy pain, allow that sad relief;
Ah, more than share it, give me all thy grief.
Heav'n first taught letters for some wretch's aid,
Some banish'd lover, or some captive maid;
They live, they speak, they breathe what love inspires,
Warm from the soul, and faithful to its fires,
The virgin's wish without her fears impart,
Excuse the blush, and pour out all the heart,
Speed the soft intercourse from soul to soul,
And waft a sigh from Indus to the Pole.

POEMS OF ALEXANDER POPE

Thou know'st how guiltless first I met thy
    flame,
When Love approach'd me under Friendship's name;
My fancy form'd thee of angelic kind,
Some emanation of th' all-beauteous Mind.
Those smiling eyes, attemp'ring ev'ry ray,
Shone sweetly lambent with celestial day.
Guiltless I gaz'd; Heaven listen'd while you sung;
And truths[1] divine came mended from that tongue.
From lips like those, what precept fail'd to move?
Too soon they taught me 'twas no sin to love:
Back through the paths of pleasing sense I ran,
Nor wish'd an Angel whom I lov'd a Man.
Dim and remote the joys of saints I see;
Nor envy them that heav'n I lose for thee.

How oft, when press'd to marriage, have I said,
Curse on all laws but those which love has made?
Love, free as air, at sight of human ties,
Spreads his light wings, and in a moment flies.
Let wealth, let honour, wait the wedded dame,
August her deed, and sacred be her fame;
Before true passion all those views remove;
Fame, wealth, and honour! what are you to Love?
The jealous God, when we profane his fires,
Those restless passions in revenge inspires,
And bids them make mistaken mortals groan,
Who seek in love for aught but love alone.
Should at my feet the world's great master fall,
Himself, his throne, his world, I'd scorn 'em all:
Not Caesar's empress would I deign to prove;
No, make me mistress to the man I love;
If there be yet another name more free,
More fond than mistress, make me that to thee!

1. He was her Preceptor in Philosophy and Divinity. *P.*

68

Oh! happy state! when souls each other draw,
When love is liberty, and nature, law:
All then is full, possessing and possess'd,
No craving void left aking in the breast:
Ev'n thought meets thought, ere from the lips it part,
And each warm wish springs mutual from the heart.
This sure is bliss (if bliss on earth there be)
And once the lot of Abelard and me.

Alas how chang'd! what sudden horrors rise!
A naked Lover bound and bleeding lies!
Where, where was Eloise? her voice, her hand!
Her poniard, had oppos'd the dire command.
Barbarian, stay! that bloody stroke restrain;
The crime was common, common be the pain.
I can no more; by shame, by rage suppress'd,
Let tears, and burning blushes speak the rest.

Canst thou forget that sad, that solemn day,
When victims at yon altar's foot we lay?
Canst thou forget what tears that moment fell,
When, warm in youth, I bade the world farewell?
As with cold lips I kiss'd the sacred veil,
The shrines all trembled, and the lamps grew pale:
Heav'n scarce believed the Conquest it survey'd,
And Saints with wonder heard the vows I made.
Yet then, to those dread altars as I drew,
Not on the Cross my eyes were fix'd, but you:
Not grace, or zeal, love only was my call,
And if I lose thy love, I lose my all.
Come! with thy looks, thy words, relieve my woe;
Those still at least are left thee to bestow.
Still on that breast enamour'd let me lie,
Still drink delicious poison from thy eye,
Pant on thy lip, and to thy heart be press'd;
Give all thou canst – and let me dream the rest.

Ah, no! instruct me other joys to prize,
With other beauties charm my partial eyes,
Full in my view set all the bright abode,
And make my soul quit Abelard for God.

Ah, think at least thy flock deserves thy care,
Plants of thy hand, and children of thy pray'r.
From the false world in early youth they fled,
By thee to mountains, wilds, and deserts led.
You[1] rais'd these hallow'd walls; the desert smil'd,
And Paradise was open'd in the Wild.
No weeping orphan saw his father's stores
Our shrines irradiate, or emblaze the floors;
No silver saints, by dying misers giv'n,
Here brib'd the rage of ill-requited Heav'n:
But such plain roofs as Piety could raise,
And only vocal with the Maker's praise.
In these lone walls (their days eternal bound)
These moss-grown domes with spiry turrets
        crown'd,
Where awful arches make a noon-day night,
And the dim windows shed a solemn light;
Thy eyes diffus'd a reconciling ray,
And gleams of glory brighten'd all the day.
But now no face divine contentment wears,
'Tis all blank sadness, or continual tears.
See how the force of others pray'rs I try,
(O pious fraud of am'rous charity!)
But why should I on others pray'rs depend?
Come thou, my father, brother, husband, friend!
Ah let thy handmaid, sister, daughter move,
And all those tender names in one, thy love!
The darksome pines that o'er yon rocks reclin'd,
Wave high, and murmur to the hollow wind,

1. He founded the Monastery. *P.*

The wand'ring streams that shine between the hills,
The grots that echo to the tinkling rills,
The dying gales that pant upon the trees,
The lakes that quiver to the curling breeze;
No more these scenes my meditation aid,
Or lull to rest the visionary maid.
But o'er the twilight groves and dusky caves,
Long-sounding aisles, and intermingled graves,
Black Melancholy sits, and round her throws
A death-like silence, and a dread repose:
Her gloomy presence saddens all the scene,
Shades ev'ry flow'r, and darkens ev'ry green,
Deepens the murmur of the falling floods,
And breathes a browner horror on the woods.

Yet here for ever, ever must I stay;
Sad proof how well a lover can obey!
Death, only death, can break the lasting chain;
And here, ev'n then, shall my cold dust remain,
Here all its frailties, all its flames resign,
And wait till 'tis no sin to mix with thine.

Ah wretch! believ'd the spouse of God in vain,
Confess'd within the slave of love and man.
Assist me, heav'n! but whence arose that pray'r?
Sprung it from piety, or from despair?
Ev'n here, where frozen chastity retires,
Love finds an altar for forbidden fires.
I ought to grieve, but cannot what I ought;
I mourn the lover, not lament the fault;
I view my crime, but kindle at the view,
Repent old pleasures, and solicit new;
Now turn'd to heav'n, I weep my past offence,
Now think of thee, and curse my innocence.
Of all affliction taught a lover yet,
'Tis sure the hardest science to forget!

How shall I lose the sin, yet keep the sense,
And love th' offender, yet detest th' offence?
How the dear object from the crime remove,
Or how distinguish penitence from love?
Unequal task! a passion to resign,
For hearts so touch'd, so pierced, so lost as mine.
Ere such a soul regains its peaceful state,
How often must it love, how often hate!
How often hope, despair, resent, regret,
Conceal, disdain, – do all things but forget.
But let heav'n seize it, all at once 'tis fir'd;
Not touch'd, but rapt; not waken'd, but inspir'd!
Oh come! oh teach me nature to subdue,
Renounce my love, my life, myself – and you.
Fill my fond heart with God alone, for he
Alone can rival, can succeed to thee.

   How happy is the blameless Vestal's lot?
The world forgetting, by the world forgot:
Eternal sunshine of the spotless mind!
Each pray'r accepted, and each wish resign'd;
Labour and rest, that equal periods keep;
'Obedient slumbers that can wake and weep;'
Desires compos'd, affections ever ev'n;
Tears that delight, and sighs that waft to heav'n.
Grace shines around her with serenest beams,
And whispering Angels prompt her golden dreams.
For her th' unfading rose of Eden blooms,
And wings of Seraphs shed divine perfumes;
For her the Spouse prepares the bridal ring,
For her white virgins Hymenaeals sing,
To sounds of heav'nly harps she dies away,
And melts in visions of eternal day.

   Far other dreams my erring soul employ,
Far other raptures, of unholy joy:

When at the close of each sad, sorrowing day,
Fancy restores what vengeance snatch'd away,
Then conscience sleeps, and leaving nature free,
All my loose soul unbounded springs to thee.
Oh curst, dear horrors of all-conscious night!
How glowing guilt exalts the keen delight!
Provoking Demons all restraint remove,
And stir within me ev'ry source of love.
I hear thee, view thee, gaze o'er all thy charms,
And round thy phantom glue my clasping arms.
I wake: — no more I hear, no more I view,
The phantom flies me, as unkind as you.
I call aloud; it hears not what I say:
I stretch my empty arms; it glides away.
To dream once more I close my willing eyes;
Ye soft illusions, dear deceits, arise;
Alas, no more! methinks we wand'ring go
Through dreary wastes, and weep each other's woe,
Where round some mould'ring tow'r pale ivy creeps,
And low-brow'd rocks hang nodding o'er the deeps.
Sudden you mount, you beckon from the skies;
Clouds interpose, waves roar, and winds arise.
I shriek, start up, the same sad prospect find,
And wake to all the griefs I left behind.

For thee the fates, severely kind, ordain
A cool suspense from pleasure and from pain;
Thy life a long dead calm of fix'd repose;
No pulse that riots, and no blood that glows.
Still as the sea, ere winds were taught to blow,
Or moving spirit bade the waters flow;
Soft as the slumbers of a saint forgiv'n,
And mild as op'ning gleams of promis'd heav'n.
Come, Abelard! for what hast thou to dread?
The torch of Venus burns not for the dead.

Nature stands check'd; Religion disapproves;
Ev'n thou art cold — yet Eloisa loves.
Ah hopeless, lasting flames; like those that burn
To light the dead, and warm th' unfruitful urn.

    What scenes appear where'er I turn my view?
The dear Ideas, where I fly, pursue,
Rise in the grove, before the altar rise,
Stain all my soul, and wanton in my eyes.
I waste the Matin lamp in sighs for thee,
Thy image steals between my God and me,
Thy voice I seem in ev'ry hymn to hear,
With ev'ry bead I drop too soft a tear.
When from the censer clouds of fragrance roll,
And swelling organs lift the rising soul,
One thought of thee puts all the pomp to flight,
Priests, tapers, temples, swim before my sight:
In seas of flame my plunging soul is drown'd,
While Altars blaze, and Angels tremble round.

    While prostrate here in humble grief I lie,
Kind, virtuous drops just gath'ring in my eye,
While praying, trembling, in the dust I roll,
And dawning grace is op'ning on my soul:
Come, if thou dar'st, all charming as thou art!
Oppose thyself to heav'n; dispute my heart;
Come, with one glance of those deluding eyes
Blot out each bright Idea of the skies;
Take back that grace, those sorrows, and those tears;
Take back my fruitless penitence and pray'rs;
Snatch me, just mounting, from the blest abode;
Assist the fiends, and tear me from my God!

    No, fly me, fly me, far as Pole from Pole;
Rise Alps between us! and whole oceans roll!
Ah, come not, write not, think not once of me,
Nor share one pang of all I felt for thee.

Thy oaths I quit, thy memory resign;
Forget, renounce me, hate whate'er was mine.
Fair eyes, and tempting looks (which yet I view!)
Long lov'd, ador'd ideas, all adieu!
O Grace serene! O virtue heav'nly fair!
Divine oblivion of low-thoughted care!
Fresh-blooming Hope, gay daughter of the sky!
And Faith, our early immortality!
Enter, each mild, each amicable guest;
Receive, and wrap me, in eternal rest!
    See in her cell sad Eloisa spread,
Propt on some tomb, a neighbour of the dead.
In each low wind methinks a Spirit calls,
And more than Echoes talk along the walls.
Here, as I watch'd the dying lamps around,
From yonder shrine I heard a hollow sound.
'Come, sister, come!' (it said, or seem'd to say)
'Thy place is here, sad sister, come away!
Once like thyself, I trembled, wept, and pray'd,
Love's victim then, tho' now a sainted maid:
But all is calm in this eternal sleep;
Here grief forgets to groan, and love to weep,
Ev'n superstition loses every fear:
For God, not man, absolves our frailties here.'
    I come, I come! prepare your roseate bow'rs,
Celestial palms, and ever-blooming flow'rs.
Thither, where sinners may have rest, I go,
Where flames refin'd in breasts seraphic glow:
Thou, Abelard! the last sad office pay,
And smooth my passage to the realms of day:
See my lips tremble, and my eye-balls roll,
Suck my last breath and catch my flying soul!
Ah no – in sacred vestments may'st thou stand,
The hallow'd taper trembling in thy hand,

Present the Cross before my lifted eye,
Teach me at once, and learn of me to die.
Ah then, thy once-lov'd Eloisa see!
It will be then no crime to gaze on me.
See from my cheek the transient roses fly!
See the last sparkle languish in my eye!
'Till every motion, pulse, and breath be o'er;
And ev'n my Abelard be lov'd no more.
O Death all-eloquent! you only prove
What dust we doat on, when 'tis man we love.

Then too, when fate shall thy fair frame destroy,
(That cause of all my guilt, and all my joy)
In trance extatic may thy pangs be drown'd,
Bright clouds descend, and Angels watch thee
   round,
From op'ning skies may streaming glories shine,
And Saints embrace thee with a love like mine.

May one kind grave[1] unite each hapless name,
And graft my love immortal on thy fame!
Then, ages hence, when all my woes are o'er,
When this rebellious heart shall beat no more;
If ever chance two wand'ring lovers brings
To Paraclete's white walls and silver springs,
O'er the pale marble shall they join their heads,
And drink the falling tears each other sheds;
Then sadly say, with mutual pity mov'd,
'Oh, may we never love as these have lov'd!'
From the full choir when loud Hosannas rise,
And swell the pomp of dreadful sacrifice,
Amid that scene if some relenting eye
Glance on the stone where our cold relics lie,

---

1. Abelard and Eloisa were interr'd in the same grave, or in monuments adjoining, in the Monastery of the Paraclete. He died in the year 1142, she in 1163. *P.*

Devotion's self shall steal a thought from heav'n,
One human tear shall drop, and be forgiv'n.
And sure if fate some future bard shall join
In sad similitude of griefs to mine,
Condemn'd whole years in absence to deplore,
And image charms he must behold no more;
Such if there be, who loves so long, so well;
Let him our sad, our tender story tell;
The well-sung woes will soothe my pensive ghost;
He best can paint 'em who shall feel 'em most.

ELEGY TO THE MEMORY OF AN
UNFORTUNATE LADY

WHAT beck'ning ghost, along the moon-light shade
Invites my steps, and points to yonder glade?
'Tis she! – but why that bleeding bosom gor'd,
Why dimly gleams the visionary sword?
Oh ever beauteous, ever friendly! tell,
Is it, in heav'n, a crime to love too well?
To bear too tender, or too firm a heart,
To act a Lover's or a Roman's part?
Is there no bright reversion in the sky,
For those who greatly think, or bravely die?

Why bade ye else, ye Pow'rs! her soul aspire
Above the vulgar flight of low desire?
Ambition first sprung from your blest abodes;
The glorious fault of Angels and of Gods:
Thence to their images on earth it flows,
And in the breasts of Kings and Heroes glows.
Most souls, 'tis true, but peep out once an age,
Dull, sullen pris'ners in the body's cage:
Dim lights of life, that burn a length of years
Useless, unseen, as lamps in sepulchres;
Like Eastern Kings a lazy state they keep,
And, close confin'd to their own palace, sleep.

From these perhaps (ere nature bade her die)
Fate snatch'd her early to the pitying sky.
As into air the purer spirits flow,
And sep'rate from their kindred dregs below;
So flew the soul to its congenial place,
Nor left one virtue to redeem her Race.

But thou, false guardian of a charge too good,
Thou, mean deserter of thy brother's blood!

See on these ruby lips the trembling breath,
These cheeks now fading at the blast of death;
Cold is that breast which warm'd the world before,
And those love-darting eyes must roll no more.
Thus, if Eternal justice rules the ball,
Thus shall your wives, and thus your children fall:
On all the line a sudden vengeance waits,
And frequent herses shall besiege your gates;
There passengers shall stand, and pointing say,
(While the long fun'rals blacken all the way)
'Lo! these were they, whose souls the Furies steel'd,
And curs'd with hearts unknowing how to yield.'
Thus unlamented pass the proud away,
The gaze of fools, and pageant of a day!
So perish all, whose breast ne'er learn'd to glow
For others good, or melt at others woe.

What can atone (Oh ever-injur'd shade!)
Thy fate unpity'd, and thy rites unpaid?
No friend's complaint, no kind domestic tear
Pleas'd thy pale ghost, or grac'd thy mournful bier.
By foreign hands thy dying eyes were clos'd,
By foreign hands thy decent limbs composed,
By foreign hands thy humble grave adorn'd,
By strangers honour'd, and by strangers mourn'd!
What tho' no friends in sable weeds appear,
Grieve for an hour, perhaps, then mourn a year,
And bear about the mockery of woe
To midnight dances, and the public show?
What tho' no weeping Loves thy ashes grace,
Nor polish'd marble emulate thy face?
What tho' no sacred earth allow thee room,
Nor hallow'd dirge be mutter'd o'er thy tomb?
Yet shall thy grave with rising flow'rs be drest,
And the green turf lie lightly on thy breast:

There shall the morn her earliest tears bestow,
There the first roses of the year shall blow;
While Angels with their silver wings o'ershade
The ground, now sacred by thy reliques made.

So peaceful rests, without a stone, a name,
What once had beauty, titles, wealth, and fame.
How lov'd, how honour'd once, avails thee not,
To whom related, or by whom begot;
A heap of dust alone remains of thee,
'Tis all thou art, and all the proud shall be!

Poets themselves must fall like those they sung,
Deaf the prais'd ear, and mute the tuneful tongue.
Ev'n he, whose soul now melts in mournful lays,
Shall shortly want the gen'rous tear he pays;
Then from his closing eyes thy form shall part,
And the last pang shall tear thee from his heart,
Life's idle business at one gasp be o'er,
The Muse forgot, and thou belov'd no more!

EPISTLE TO MRS BLOUNT[1]

WITH THE WORKS OF VOITURE[2]

In these gay thoughts the Loves and Graces shine,
And all the Writer lives in ev'ry line;
His easy Art may happy Nature seem,
Trifles themselves are elegant in him.
Sure to charm all was his peculiar fate,
Who without flatt'ry pleased the fair and great;
Still with esteem no less convers'd than read;
With wit well-natur'd, and with books well-bred:
His heart, his mistress, and his friend did share,
His time, the Muse, the witty, and the fair.
Thus wisely careless, innocently gay,
Chearful he play'd the trifle, Life, away;
Till fate scarce felt his gentle breath supprest,
As smiling Infants sport themselves to rest.
Ev'n rival Wits did Voiture's death deplore,
And the gay mourn'd who never mourn'd before;
The truest hearts for Voiture heav'd with sighs,
Voiture was wept by all the brightest Eyes:
The Smiles and Loves had dy'd in Voiture's death,
But that for ever in his lines they breathe.

Let the strict life of graver mortals be
A long, exact, and serious Comedy;
In ev'ry scene some Moral let it teach,
And, if it can, at once both please and preach.
Let mine an innocent gay Farce appear,
And more diverting still than regular,

1. This poem was addressed to Martha Blount (1690–1762), a life-
long and intimate friend of Pope's. He also addressed verses to her
sister, Teresa.
2. Vincent Voiture (1598–1648); a French wit and letter writer.

Have Humour, Wit, a native Ease and Grace,
Tho' not too strictly bound to Time and Place:
Critics in Wit, or Life, are hard to please,
Few write to those, and none can live to these.

   Too much your Sex is by their forms confin'd,
Severe to all, but most to Womankind;
Custom, grown blind with Age, must be your guide;
Your pleasure is a vice, but not your pride;
By Nature yielding, stubborn but for fame;
Made Slaves by honour, and made Fools by shame.
Marriage may all those petty Tyrants chase,
But sets up one, a greater in their place:
Well might you wish for change by those accurst,
But the last Tyrant ever proves the worst.
Still in constraint your suff'ring Sex remains,
Or bound in formal, or in real chains:
Whole years neglected, for some months ador'd,
The fawning Servant turns a haughty Lord.
Ah quit not the free innocence of life,
For the dull glory of a virtuous Wife;
Nor let false Shews, or empty Titles please:
Aim not at Joy, but rest content with Ease.

   The Gods, to curse Pamela with her pray'rs,
Gave the gilt Coach and dappled Flanders Mares,
The shining robes, rich jewels, beds of state,
And, to complete her bliss, a Fool for Mate.
She glares in Balls, front Boxes, and the Ring,
A vain, unquiet, glitt'ring, wretched Thing!
Pride, Pomp, and State but reach her outward part:
She sighs, and is no Duchess at her heart.

   But, Madam, if the Fates withstand, and you
Are destin'd Hymen's willing Victim too:
Trust not too much your now resistless charms,
Those, Age or Sickness, soon or late, disarms:

Good-humour only teaches charms to last
Still makes new conquests, and maintains the past;
Love, rais'd on Beauty, will like that decay,
Our hearts may bear its slender chain a day;
As flow'ry bands in wantonness are worn,
A morning's pleasure, and at evening torn;
This binds in ties more easy, yet more strong,
The willing heart, and only holds it long.

    Thus Voiture's early care still shone the same,
And Monthausier[1] was only chang'd in name:
By this, ev'n now they live, ev'n now they charm,
Their Wit still sparkling, and their flames still warm.

    Now crown'd with Myrtle, on th' Elysian coast,
Amid those Lovers, joys his gentle Ghost:
Pleas'd, while with smiles his happy lines you view,
And finds a fairer Rambouillet[1] in you.
The brightest eyes of France inspir'd his Muse;
The brightest eyes of Britain now peruse;
And dead, as living, 'tis our Author's pride
Still to charm those who charm the world beside.

1. Madame de Monthausier was the name under which Voiture celebrated Mlle de Rambouillet.

EPISTLE TO MRS TERESA BLOUNT[1]

ON HER LEAVING THE TOWN AFTER
THE CORONATION[2]

As some fond Virgin, whom her mother's care
Drags from the Town to wholesome Country air,
Just when she learns to roll a melting eye,
And hear a spark, yet think no danger nigh;
From the dear man unwilling she must sever,
Yet takes one kiss before she parts for ever:
Thus from the world fair Zephalinda flew,
Saw others happy, and with sighs withdrew;
Not that their pleasures caus'd her discontent,
She sigh'd not that they stay'd, but that she went.

She went, to plain-work, and to purling brooks,
Old-fashion'd halls, dull Aunts, and croaking rooks:
She went from Op'ra, Park, Assembly, Play,
To morning-walks, and pray'rs three hours a-day;
To part her time 'twixt reading and bohea,
To muse, and spill her solitary tea,
Or o'er cold coffee trifle with the spoon,
Count the slow clock, and dine exact at noon:
Divert her eyes with pictures in the fire,
Hum half a tune, tell stories to the squire;
Up to her godly garret after sev'n,
There starve and pray, for that's the way to heav'n.

Some Squire, perhaps, you take delight to rack;
Whose game is Whisk, whose treat a toast in sack;
Who visits with a Gun, presents you birds,
Then gives a smacking buss, and cries, – No words!
Or with his hound comes hallooing from the stable,
Makes love with nods, and knees beneath a table;

1. See p. 81, n. 1.   2. Of King George I. 1715. *P.*

Whose laughs are hearty, tho' his jests are coarse,
And loves you best of all things – but his horse.

In some fair ev'ning, on your elbow laid,
You dream of Triumphs in the rural shade;
In pensive thought recall the fancy'd scene,
See Coronations rise on ev'ry green;
Before you pass th' imaginary sights
Of Lords, and Earls, and Dukes, and garter'd Knights,
While the spread fan o'ershades your closing eyes;
Then give one flirt, and all the vision flies.
Thus vanish sceptres, coronets, and balls,
And leave you in lone woods, or empty walls!

So when your Slave, at some dear idle time,
(Not plagu'd with head-achs, or the want of rhyme)
Stands in the streets, abstracted from the crew,
And while he seems to study, thinks of you;
Just when his fancy paints your sprightly eyes,
Or sees the blush of soft Parthenia rise,
Gay[1] pats my shoulder, and you vanish quite,
Streets, Chairs, and Coxcombs rush upon my sight;
Vex'd to be still in town, I knit my brow,
Look sour, and hum a Tune, as you do now

1. John Gay (1685-1732); poet and a friend of Pope's.

EPISTLE TO MR JERVAS[1]

WITH MR DRYDEN'S TRANSLATION OF FRESNOY'S 'ART OF PAINTING'[2]

THIS Verse be thine, my friend, nor thou refuse
This, from no venal or ungrateful Muse.
Whether thy hand strike out some free design,
Where Life awakes, and dawns at ev'ry line;
Or blend in beauteous tints the colour'd mass,
And from the canvas call the mimic face:
Read these instructive leaves, in which conspire
Fresnoy's close Art, and Dryden's native Fire:
And reading wish, like theirs, our fate and fame,
So mix'd our studies, and so join'd our name;
Like them to shine through long succeeding age,
So just thy skill, so regular my rage.

Smit with the love of Sister-Arts we came,
And met congenial, mingling flame with flame;
Like friendly colours found them both unite,
And each from each contract new strength and light.
How oft' in pleasing tasks we wear the day,
While summer-suns roll unperceiv'd away?
How oft our slowly-growing works impart,
While Images reflect from art to art?
How oft review; each finding like a friend
Something to blame, and something to commend?

What flatt'ring scenes our wand'ring fancy wrought,
Rome's pompous glories rising to our thought!
Together o'er the Alps methinks we fly
Fir'd with Ideas of fair Italy.

1. Charles Jervas (1675–1739); a fashionable portrait painter who taught painting to Pope.
2. John Dryden translated Charles Fresnoy's (1613–65) Latin poem, *The Art of Painting*.

With thee, on Raphael's Monument I mourn,
Or wait inspiring Dreams at Maro's Urn:
With thee repose, where Tully once was laid,
Or seek some Ruin's formidable shade:
While Fancy brings the vanish'd piles to view,
And builds imaginary Rome a-new,
Here thy well-study'd marbles fix our eye;
A fading Fresco here demands a sigh:
Each heav'nly piece unwearied we compare,
Match Raphael's grace with thy lov'd Guido's air,
Carracci's strength, Correggio's softer line,
Paulo's free stroke, and Titian's warmth divine.

How finish'd with illustrious toil appears
This small, well-polish'd Gem, the work of years![1]
Yet still how faint by precept is exprest
The living image in the painter's breast?
Thence endless streams of fair Ideas flow,
Strike in the sketch, or in the picture glow;
Thence Beauty, waking all her forms, supplies
An Angel's sweetness, or Bridgewater's eyes.[2]

Muse! at that Name thy sacred sorrows shed,
Those tears eternal, that embalm the dead:
Call round her Tomb each object of desire,
Each purer frame inform'd with purer fire:
Bid her be all that chears or softens life,
The tender sister, daughter, friend, and wife:
Bid her be all that makes mankind adore;
Then view this Marble, and be vain no more!

Yet still her charms in breathing paint engage;
Her modest cheek shall warm a future age.

---

1. Fresnoy employed above twenty years in finishing this poem. *P.*
2. Elizabeth, Countess of Bridgewater, the third daughter of the Duke
   of Marlborough, who died in 1714 of the small-pox, aged 27.

Beauty, frail flow'r that ev'ry season fears,
Blooms in thy colours for a thousand years.
Thus Churchill's race shall other hearts surprise,
And other Beauties envy Worsley's eyes.[1]
Each pleasing Blount[2] shall endless smiles bestow,
And soft Belinda's[3] blush for ever glow.

   Oh lasting as those Colours may they shine,
Free as thy stroke, yet faultless as thy line;
New graces yearly like thy works display,
Soft without weakness, without glaring gay;
Led by some rule, that guides, but not constrains;
And finish'd more through happiness than pains.
The kindred Arts shall in their praise conspire,
One dip the pencil, and one string the lyre.
Yet should the Graces all thy figures place,
And breathe an air divine on ev'ry face;
Yet should the Muses bid my numbers roll
Strong as their charms, and gentle as their soul;
With Zeuxis' Helen thy Bridgewater vie,
And these be sung till Granville's Myra die:[4]
Alas! how little from the grave we claim!
Thou but preserv'st a Face, and I a Name.

---

1. Frances, Lady Worsley, wife of Sir Robert Worsley, Bart.
2. See p. 81, n. 1.   3. Miss Fermor; see p. 39, n. 1.
4. George Granville, Lord Lansdowne (1665–1735) – a friend of
Pope's – addressed love verses to *Myra*.

EPISTLE TO ROBERT EARL OF OXFORD
AND EARL MORTIMER[1]

Such were the notes thy once-lov'd Poet sung,
Till Death untimely.stop'd his tuneful tongue.
Oh just beheld, and lost! admir'd and mourn'd!
With softest manners, gentlest arts adorn'd!
Blest in each science, blest in ev'ry strain!
Dear to the Muse! to HARLEY dear – in vain!

For him, thou oft hast bid the World attend,
Fond to forget the Statesman in the Friend;
For SWIFT[2] and him, despis'd the farce of state,
The sober follies of the wise and great;
Dext'rous, the craving, fawning crowd to quit,
And pleas'd to 'scape from Flattery to Wit.

Absent or dead, still let a friend be dear,
(A sigh the absent claims, the dead a tear)
Recall those nights that clos'd thy toilsome days,
Still hear thy Parnell in his living lays,
Who, careless now of Int'rest, Fame, or Fate,
Perhaps forgets that OXFORD e'er was great;
Or deeming meanest what we greatest call,
Beholds thee glorious only in thy Fall.

And sure, if aught below the seats divine
Can touch Immortals, 'tis a Soul like thine:
A Soul supreme, in each hard instance try'd,
Above all Pain, all Passion, and all Pride,

1. This Epistle was sent to the Earl of Oxford [1661–1724] with Dr Parnell's [1679–1718] Poems, published by our author, after the said Earl's imprisonment in the Tower [he was confined there from 1714–17 after falling from political power], and retreat into the country in the year 1721. *P.*
2. Jonathan Swift (1667–1745); the great satirist and friend of Pope's.

The rage of Pow'r, the blast of public breath,
The lust of Lucre, and the dread of Death.
　　In vain to Deserts thy retreat is made;
The Muse attends thee to thy silent shade:
'Tis hers the brave man's latest steps to trace,
Rejudge his acts, and dignify disgrace.
When Int'rest calls off all her sneaking train,
And all th' oblig'd desert, and all the vain;
She waits, or to the scaffold, or the cell,
When the last ling'ring friend has bid farewell.
Ev'n now, she shades thy Ev'ning-walk with bays,
(No hireling she, no prostitute to praise)
Ev'n now, observant of the parting ray,
Eyes the calm Sun-set of thy various Day,
Through Fortune's cloud one truly great can see,
Nor fears to tell, that MORTIMER is he.

EPITAPHS

ON THE HON. SIMON HARCOURT, ONLY SON OF THE
LORD CHANCELLOR HARCOURT; AT THE CHURCH OF
STANTON HARCOURT IN OXFORDSHIRE, 1720

To this sad Shrine, whoe'er thou art! draw near,
Here lies the Friend most lov'd, the Son most dear:
Who ne'er knew Joy, but Friendship might divide,
Or gave his Father Grief but when he dy'd.
　　How vain is Reason, Eloquence how weak!
If *Pope* must tell what HARCOURT cannot speak.
Oh, let thy once-lov'd Friend inscribe thy Stone,
And, with a Father's sorrows, mix his own!

ON MRS CORBET, WHO DIED OF A CANCER
IN HER BREAST

HERE rests a Woman, good without pretence,
Blest with plain Reason, and with sober Sense:
No Conquests she, but o'er herself, desir'd,
No Arts essay'd, but not to be admir'd.
Passion and Pride were to her soul unknown,
Convinc'd that Virtue only is our own.
So unaffected, so compos'd a mind;
So firm, yet soft; so strong, yet so refin'd;
Heav'n, as its purest gold, by Tortures try'd!
The Saint sustain'd it, but the Woman died.

ON SIR WILLIAM TRUMBAL[1]

A PLEASING Form; a firm, yet cautious Mind;
Sincere, tho' prudent; constant, yet resign'd:

1. See p. 1, n. 1.

Honour unchang'd, a Principle profest,
Fix'd to one side, but mod'rate to the rest:
An honest Courtier, yet a Patriot too;
Just to his Prince, and to his Country true:
Fill'd with the Sense of Age, the Fire of Youth,
A Scorn of Wrangling, yet a Zeal for Truth;
A gen'rous Faith, from Superstition free;
A Love to Peace, and Hate of Tyranny;
Such this Man was; who now, from earth remov'd,
At length enjoys that Liberty he lov'd.

ON MR GAY, IN WESTMINSTER-ABBEY, 1732[1]

OF Manners gentle, of Affections mild;
In Wit, a Man; Simplicity, a Child:
With native Humour temp'ring virtuous Rage,
Form'd to delight at once and lash the age:
Above Temptation, in a low Estate,
And uncorrupted, ev'n among the Great:
A safe Companion, and an easy Friend,
Unblam'd through Life, lamented in thy End.
These are Thy Honours! not that here thy Bust
Is mix'd with Heroes, or with Kings thy dust;
But that the Worthy and the Good shall say,
Striking their pensive bosoms – *Here* lies GAY.

INTENDED FOR SIR ISAAC NEWTON, IN WESTMINSTER-ABBEY

NATURE and Nature's Laws lay hid in Night:
GOD said, *Let Newton be!* and all was Light.

1. See p. 85, n. 1.

ODE ON SOLITUDE[1]

HAPPY the man, whose wish and care
   A few paternal acres bound,
Content to breathe his native air,
         In his own ground.

Whose herds with milk, whose fields with bread,
   Whose flocks supply him with attire,
Whose trees in summer yield him shade,
         In winter fire.

Blest, who can unconcern'dly find
   Hours, days, and years slide soft away,
In health of body, peace of mind,
         Quiet by day,

Sound sleep by night; study and ease,
   Together mixt; sweet recreation;
And innocence, which most does please
         With meditation.

Thus let me live, unseen, unknown,
   Thus unlamented let me die,
Steal from the world, and not a stone
         Tell where I lie.

1. This was a very early production of our Author, written about
twelve years old. *P.*

ON SILENCE[1]

I

SILENCE! coeval with Eternity;
Thou wert, ere Nature's self began to be,
'Twas one vast Nothing, all, and all slept fast in thee.

II

Thine was the sway, ere heav'n was form'd, or
earth,
Ere fruitful Thought conceiv'd Creation's birth,
Or midwife Word gave aid, and spoke the infant forth.

III

Then various elements, against thee join'd,
In one more various animal combin'd,
And fram'd the clam'rous race of busy humankind.

IV

The tongue mov'd gently first, and speech was low,
Till wrangling Science taught it noise and show,
And wicked Wit arose, thy most abusive foe.

V

But rebel Wit deserts thee oft' in vain;
Lost in the maze of words he turns again,
And seeks a surer state, and courts thy gentle reign.

1. This is an imitation of the Earl of Rochester's (1648-80) verses
On Nothing.

94

VI

Afflicted Sense thou kindly dost set free,
    Oppress'd with argumental tyranny,
And routed Reason finds a safe retreat in thee.

VII

With thee in private modest Dulness lies,
    And in thy bosom lurks in Thought's disguise;
Thou varnisher of Fools, and cheat of all the Wise!

VIII

Yet thy indulgence is by both confest;
    Folly by thee lies sleeping in the breast,
And 'tis in thee at last that Wisdom seeks for rest.

IX

Silence! the knave's repute, the whore's good name,
    The only honour of the wishing dame;
Thy very want of tongue makes thee a kind of Fame.

X

But could'st thou seize some tongues that now are
        free,
    How Church and State should be oblig'd to thee!
At Senate, and at Bar, how welcome would'st thou be!

XI

Yet speech ev'n there, submissively withdraws
    From rights of subjects, and the poor man's cause:
Then pompous Silence reigns, and stills the noisy
        Laws.

XII

Past services of friends, good deeds of foes,
    What Fav'rites gain, and what the Nation owes,
Fly the forgetful world, and in thy arms repose.

XIII

The country wit, religion of the town,
    The courtier's learning, policy o' th' gown,
Are best by thee express'd; and shine in thee alone.

XIV

The parson's cant, the lawyer's sophistry,
    Lord's quibble, critic's jest; all end in thee,
All rest in peace at last, and sleep eternally.

THE DYING CHRISTIAN
TO HIS SOUL

I

VITAL spark of heav'nly flame!
Quit, oh quit this mortal frame:
Trembling, hoping, ling'ring, flying,
Oh the pain, the bliss of dying!
Cease, fond Nature, cease thy strife,
And let me languish into life.

II

Hark! they whisper; Angels say,
'Sister Spirit, come away!'
What is this absorbs me quite?
Steals my senses, shuts my sight,
Drowns my spirits, draws my breath?
Tell me, my Soul, can this be Death?

III

The world recedes; it disappears!
Heav'n opens on my eyes! my ears
With sounds seraphic ring:
Lend, lend your wings! I mount! I fly!
O Grave! where is thy Victory?
O Death! where is thy Sting?

TO THE AUTHOR OF A POEM
ENTITLED SUCCESSIO[1]

Begone, ye critics, and restrain your spite,
Codrus writes on, and will for ever write.
The heaviest Muse the swiftest course has gone,
As clocks run fastest when most lead is on;
What though no bees around your cradle flew,
Nor on your lips distill'd the golden dew,
Yet have we oft discover'd in their stead
A swarm of drones that buzz'd about your head.
When you, like *Orpheus*, strike the warbling lyre,
Attentive blocks stand round you and admire.
Wit pass'd thro' thee no longer is the same,
As meat digested takes a diff'rent name,
But sense must sure thy safest plunder be,
Since no reprisals can be made on thee.
Thus thou may'st rise, and in thy daring flight
(Though ne'er so weighty) reach a wondrous height.
So, forc'd from engines, lead itself can fly,
And ponderous slugs move nimbly thro' the sky.
Sure *Bavius* copy'd *Maevius* to the full,
And *Chaerilus* taught *Codrus* to be dull;
Therefore, dear friend, at my advice give o'er
This needless labour; and contend no more
To prove a dull *Succession* to be true,
Since 'tis enough we find it so in you.

---

1. The author was the dull poet, Elkanah Settle (1648–1724).

PROLOGUE TO MR ADDISON'S
TRAGEDY OF CATO[1]

To wake the soul by tender strokes of art,
To raise the genius, and to mend the heart,
To make mankind, in conscious virtue bold,
Live o'er each scene, and be what they behold:
For this the Tragic Muse first trod the stage,
Commanding tears to stream through ev'ry age;
Tyrants no more their savage nature kept,
And foes to virtue wonder'd how they wept.
Our author shuns by vulgar springs to move
The hero's glory, or the virgin's love;
In pitying Love, we but our weakness show,
And wild Ambition well deserves its woe.
Here tears shall flow from a more gen'rous cause,
Such tears as Patriots shed for dying Laws:
He bids your breasts with ancient ardour rise,
And calls forth Roman drops from British eyes.
Virtue confess'd in human shape he draws,
What Plato thought, and godlike Cato was:
No common object to your sight displays,
But what with pleasure Heav'n itself surveys,
A brave man struggling in the storms of fate,
And greatly falling with a falling state.
While Cato gives his little Senate laws,
What bosom beats not in his Country's cause?
Who sees him act, but envies ev'ry deed?
Who hears him groan, and does not wish to bleed?
Ev'n when proud Caesar 'midst triumphal cars,
The spoils of nations, and the pomp of wars,

1. Joseph Addison's (1672–1719) famous tragedy of *Cato* was first
acted in 1713.

Ignobly vain, and impotently great,
Show'd Rome her Cato's figure drawn in state;
As her dead Father's rev'rend image pass'd,
The pomp was darken'd and the day o'ercast;
The Triumph ceas'd, tears gush'd from ev'ry eye;
The World's great Victor pass'd unheeded by;
Her last good man dejected Rome ador'd,
And honour'd Caesar's less than Cato's sword.

   Britons, attend: be worth like this approv'd,
And show, you have the virtue to be mov'd.
With honest scorn the first fam'd Cato view'd
Rome learning arts from Greece, whom she subdued;
Your scene precariously subsists too long
On French translation, and Italian song.
Dare to have sense yourselves; assert the stage,
Be justly warm'd with your own native rage;
Such Plays alone should win a British ear,
As Cato's self had not disdain'd to hear.

EPIGRAM

I AM His Highness' dog at Kew;
Pray tell me, sir, whose dog are you?

TO MRS M. B.[1] ON HER BIRTHDAY

Oh be thou blest with all that Heav'n can send,
Long Health, long Youth, long Pleasure, and a Friend:
Not with those Toys the female world admire,
Riches that vex, and Vanities that tire.
With added years if Life bring nothing new,
But like a Sieve let ev'ry blessing through,
Some joy still lost, as each vain year runs o'er,
And all we gain, some sad Reflection more;
Is that a Birth-day? 'tis alas! too clear
'Tis but the Fun'ral of the former year.

Let Joy or Ease, let Affluence or Content,
And the gay Conscience of a life well spent,
Calm ev'ry thought, inspirit ev'ry grace,
Glow in thy heart, and smile upon thy face.
Let day improve on day, and year on year,
Without a Pain, a Trouble, or a Fear;
Till Death unfelt that tender frame destroy,
In some soft Dream, or Ecstasy of Joy,
Peaceful sleep out the Sabbath of the Tomb,
And wake to Raptures in a Life to come.

1. See p. 81, n. 1.

ON A CERTAIN LADY AT COURT

I KNOW the thing that's most uncommon;
  (Envy be silent, and attend!)
I know a reasonable Woman,
  Handsome and witty, yet a Friend.

Not warp'd by Passion, aw'd by Rumour,
  Not grave through Pride, or gay through Folly,
An equal Mixture of good Humour,
  And sensible soft Melancholy.

'Has she no faults, then (Envy says) Sir?'
  Yes, she has one, I must aver:
When all the World conspires to praise her,
  The Woman's deaf, and does not hear.

THE ILIAD

Hector and Andromache

Hector, this heard, return'd without Delay;
Swift thro' the Town he trod his former way,
Thro' Streets of Palaces and Walks of State;
And met the Mourner at the *Scæan* Gate.
With haste to meet him sprung the joyful Fair,
His blameless Wife, *Aëtion's* wealthy Heir:
(*Cilician Thebè* great *Aëtion* sway'd,
And *Hippoplacus'* wide-extended Shade)
The Nurse stood near, in whose Embraces prest
His only Hope hung smiling at her Breast,
Whom each soft Charm and early Grace adorn,
Fair as the new-born Star that gilds the Morn.
To this lov'd Infant *Hector* gave the Name
Scamandrius, from *Scamander's* honour'd Stream;
Astyanax the *Trojans* call'd the Boy,
From his great Father, the Defence of *Troy*.
Silent the Warrior smil'd, and pleas'd resign'd
To tender Passions all his mighty Mind:
His beauteous Princess cast a mournful Look,
Hung on his Hand, and then dejected spoke;
Her Bosom labour'd with a boding Sigh,
And the big Tear stood trembling in her Eye.

'Too daring Prince! ah whither dost thou run?
Ah too forgetful of thy Wife and Son!
And think'st thou not how wretched we shall be,
A Widow I, an helpless Orphan He!
For sure such Courage Length of Life denies,
And thou must fall, thy Virtue's Sacrifice.

Greece in her single Heroes strove in vain;
Now Hosts oppose thee, and thou must be slain!
Oh grant me Gods! e're *Hector* meets his Doom,
All I can ask of Heav'n, an early Tomb!

'So shall my Days in one sad Tenor run,
And end with Sorrows as they first begun.
No Parent now remains, my Griefs to share,
No father's Aid, no Mother's tender Care.
The fierce *Achilles* wrapt our Walls in Fire,
Lay'd *Thebé* waste, and slew my warlike Sire!
His fate Compassion in the Victor bred;
Stern as he was, he yet rever'd the Dead,
His radiant Arms preserv'd from hostile Spoil,
And lay'd him decent on the Fun'ral Pyle;
Then raised a Mountain where his Bones were burn'd,
The Mountain Nymphs the rural Tomb adorn'd,
Jove's Sylvan Daughters bade their Elms bestow
A barren Shade, and in his Honour grow.

'By the same Arm my sev'n brave Brothers fell,
In one sad Day beheld the Gates of Hell;
While the fat Herds and Snowie Flocks they fed,
Amid their Fields the hapless Heroes bled!
My Mother liv'd to bear the Victor's Bands,
The Queen of *Hippoplacia's* Sylvan Lands:
Redeem'd too late, she scarce beheld again
Her pleasing Empire and her native Plain,
When ah! opprest by Life-consuming woe,
She fell a victim to *Diana's* Bow.

'Yet while my *Hector* still survives, I see
My Father, Mother, Brethren, all, in thee.
Alas! my Parents, Brothers, Kindred, all,
Once more will perish if my *Hector* fall.
Thy Wife, thy Infant, in thy Danger share:
Oh prove a Husband's and a Father's Care!

That Quarter most the skillful *Greeks* annoy,
Where yon' wild Fig-Trees join the Wall of *Troy*:
Thou, from this Tow'r defend th' important Post;
There *Agamemnon* points his dreadful Host,
That Pass *Tydides*, *Ajax* strive to gain
And there the vengeful *Spartan* fires his Train.
Thrice our bold Foes the fierce Attack have giv'n,
Or led by Hopes, or dictated from Heav'n.
Let others in the Field their Arms employ,
But stay my *Hector* here, and guard his *Troy*.'

    The Chief reply'd: 'That Post shall be my Care;
Nor that alone, but all the Works of War.
How would the Sons of *Troy*, in Arms renown'd,
And *Troy's* proud Dames whose Garments sweep the
     Ground,
Attaint the Lustre of my former Name,
Should *Hector* basely quit the Field of Fame?
My early Youth was bred to martial Pains,
My Soul impells me to th' embattel'd Plains;
Let me be foremost to defend the Throne,
And guard my Father's Glories, and my own.

    'Yet come it will, the Day decreed by Fates;
(How my Heart trembles while my Tongue
     relates!)
The Day when thou, Imperial *Troy*! must bend,
And see thy Warriors fall; thy Glories end.
And yet no dire Presage so wounds my Mind,
My Mother's Death, the Ruin of my Kind,
Not *Priam's* hoary Hairs defil'd with Gore,
Not all my Brothers gasping on the Shore;
As thine, *Andromache*! thy Griefs I dread;
I see thee trembling, weeping, Captive led!
In Argive Looms our Battels to design,
And Woes, of which so large a Part was thine!

THE ILIAD

To bear the Victor's hard Commands, or bring
The Weight of Waters from *Hyperia's* Spring.
There, while you groan beneath the Load of Life,
They cry, Behold the mighty *Hector's* Wife!
Some haughty *Greek* who lives thy Tears to see,
Embitters all thy Woes, by naming me.
The Thoughts of Glory past, and present Shame,
A thousand Griefs shall waken at the Name!
May I lie cold before that dreadful Day,
Press'd with a Load of Monumental Clay!
Thy *Hector* wrapt in everlasting Sleep,
Shall neither hear thee sigh, nor see thee weep.'

Thus having spoke, th' illustrious Chief of *Troy*
Stretch'd his fond Arms to clasp the lovely Boy.
The Babe clung crying to his Nurse's Breast,
Scar'd at the dazling Helm, and nodding Crest.
With secret Pleasure each fond Parent smil'd,
And *Hector* hasted to relieve his Child,
The glitt'ring Terrors from his Brows unbound,
And plac'd the beaming Helmet on the Ground.
Then kist the Child, and lifting high in Air,
Thus to the Gods prefer'd a Father's Pray'r.

'O Thou! whose Glory fills th' Aetherial Throne
And all ye deathless Pow'rs! protect my Son!
Grant him, like me, to purchase just Renown,
To guard the *Trojans*, to defend the Crown,
Against his Country's Foes the War to wage,
And rise the *Hector* of the future Age!
So when triumphant from successful Toils,
Of Heroes slain he bears the reeking Spoils,
Whole Hosts may hail him with deserv'd Acclaim,
And say, "This Chief transcends his Father's Fame":
While pleas'd amidst the gen'ral Shouts of *Troy*,
His Mother's conscious Heart o'erflows with Joy.'

107

He spoke, and fondly gazing on her Charms
Restor'd the pleasing Burden to her Arms;
Soft on her fragrant Breast the Babe she laid,
Hush'd to Repose, and with a Smile survey'd.
The troubled Pleasure soon chastis'd by Fear,
She mingled with the Smile a tender Tear.
The soften'd Chief with kind Compassion view'd,
And dry'd the falling Drops, and thus pursu'd.
'*Andromache!* my Soul's far better Part,
Why with untimely Sorrows heaves thy Heart?
No hostile Hand can antedate my Doom,
Till Fate condemns me to the silent Tomb.
Fix'd is the Term to all the Race of Earth,
And such the hard Condition of our Birth.
No Force can then resist, no Flight can save,
All sink alike, the Fearful and the Brave.
No more – but hasten to thy Tasks at home,
There guide the Spindle, and direct the Loom:
Me Glory summons to the martial Scene,
The Field of Combat is the Sphere for Men
Where Heroes war, the foremost Place I claim,
The first in Danger as the first in Fame.'

Thus having said, the glorious Chief resumes
His Tow'ry Helmet, black with shading Plumes.
His Princess parts with a prophetick Sigh,
Unwilling parts, and oft' reverts her eye
That stream'd at ev'ry Look: then, moving slow,
Sought her own Palace, and indulg'd her Woe.
There, while her Tears deplor'd the Godlike Man,
Thro' all her Train the soft Infection ran,
The pious Maids their mingled Sorrows shed,
And mourn the living *Hector*, as the dead.

Fires at Night

THE Troops exulting sate in order round,
And beaming Fires illumin'd all the Ground.
As when the Moon, refulgent Lamp of Night!
O'er Heav'ns clear Azure sheds her sacred Light,
When not a Breath disturbs the deep Serene;
And not a Cloud o'ercasts the solemn Scene;
Around her Throne the vivid Planets roll,
And Stars unnumber'd gild the glowing Pole,
O'er the dark Trees a yellower Verdure shed,
And tip with Silver ev'ry Mountain's Head;
Then shine the Vales, the Rocks in Prospect rise,
A Flood of Glory bursts from all the Skies:
The conscious Swains, rejoicing in the Sight,
Eye the blue vault, and bless the useful Light.
So many Flames before proud *Ilion* blaze,
And lighten glimm'ring *Xanthus* with their Rays.
The long Reflections of the distant Fires
Gleam on the Walls, and tremble on the Spires.
A thousand Piles the dusky Horrors gild,
And shoot a shady Lustre o'er the Field.
Full fifty Guards each flaming Pile attend,
Whose umber'd Arms, by fits, thick Flashes send.
Loud neigh the Coursers o'er their Heaps of
    Corn,
And ardent Warriors wait the rising Morn.

Vulcan Forges a Shield for Achilles

THUS having said, the Father of the Fires
To the black Labours of his Forge retires.

Soon as he bade them blow, the Bellows turn'd
Their iron Mouths; and where the Furnace burn'd,
Resounding breath'd: At once the Blast expires
And twenty Forges catch at once the Fires;
Just as the God directs, now loud, now low,
They raise a Tempest, or they gently blow.
In hissing Flames huge silver Bars are roll'd,
And stubborn Brass, and Tin, and solid Gold:
Before, deep fix'd, th' eternal Anvils stand;
The pond'rous Hammer loads his better Hand,
His left with Tongs turns the vex'd Metal round;
And thick, strong Strokes, the doubling Vaults
    rebound.

Then first he form'd th' immense and solid *Shield*;
Rich, various Artifice emblaz'd the Field;
Its utmost verge a threefold Circle bound;
A silver Chain suspends the massy Round,
Five ample Plates the broad Expanse compose,
And god-like Labours on the Surface rose.
There shone the Image of the Master Mind:
There Earth, there Heav'n, there Ocean he design'd;
Th' unweary'd Sun, the Moon compleatly round;
The starry Lights that Heav'ns high Convex
    crown'd;
The *Pleiads*, *Hyads*, with the Northern Team;
And great *Orion's* more refulgent Beam;
To which, around the Axle of the Sky,
The *Bear* revolving, points his golden Eye,
Still shines exalted on th' aetherial Plain,
Nor bends his blazing Forehead to the Main.

Two Cities radiant on the Shield appear,
The Image one of Peace, and one of War.
Here sacred Pomp, and genial Feast delight,
And solemn Dance, and *Hymenaeal* Rite;

Along the Street the new-made Brides are led,
With Torches flaming, to the nuptial Bed;
The youthful Dancers in a Circle bound
To the soft Flute, and Cittern's silver Sound:
Thro' the fair Streets, the Matrons in a Row,
Stand in their Porches, and enjoy the Show.

   There, in the *Forum* swarm a num'rous Train;
The subject of Debate, a Townsman slain:
One pleads the Fine discharg'd, which one deny'd,
And bade the Publick and the Laws decide:
The Witness is produc'd on either Hand;
For this, or that, the partial People stand:
Th' appointed Heralds still the noisy Bands,
And form a Ring, with Scepters in their Hands;
On Seats of Stone, within the sacred Place,
The rev'rend Elders nodded o'er the Case;
Alternate, each th' attesting Scepter took,
And rising solemn, each his Sentence spoke.
Two golden Talents lay amidst, in sight,
The Prize of him who best adjudg'd the Right.

   Another Part (a Prospect diff'ring far)
Glow'd with refulgent Arms, and horrid War.
Two mighty Hosts a leaguer'd Town embrace,
And one would pillage, one wou'd burn the Place.
Meantime the Townsmen, arm'd with silent Care,
A secret Ambush on the Foe prepare:
Their Wives, their Children, and the watchful Band,
Of trembling Parents on the Turrets stand.
They march; by *Pallas* and by *Mars* made bold;
Gold were the Gods, their radiant Garments Gold,
And Gold their Armour: These the Squadron led,
August, Divine, Superior by the Head!
A Place for Ambush fit, they found, and stood
Cover'd with Shields, beside a silver Flood.

Two Spies at distance lurk, and watchful seem
If Sheep or Oxen seek the winding Stream.
Soon the white Flocks proceeded o'er the Plains,
And Steers slow-moving, and two Shepherd Swains;
Behind them, piping on their Reeds, they go,
Nor fear an Ambush, nor suspect a Foe.
In Arms the glitt'ring Squadron rising round
Rush sudden; Hills of Slaughter heap the Ground,
Whole Flocks and Herds lye bleeding on the Plains,
And, all amidst them, dead, the Shepherd Swains!
The bellowing Oxen the Besiegers hear;
They rise, take Horse, approach, and meet the War;
They fight, they fall, beside the silver Flood;
The waving Silver seem'd to blush with Blood.
There Tumult, there Contention stood confest;
One rear'd a Dagger at a Captive's Breast,
One held a living Foe, that freshly bled
With new-made Wounds; another dragg'd a dead;
Now here, now there, the Carcasses they tore:
Fate stalk'd amidst them, grim with human Gore.
And the whole War came out, and met the Eye;
And each bold Figure seem'd to live, or die.

A Field deep-furrow'd, next the God design'd,
The third time labour'd by the sweating Hind;
The shining Shares full many Plowmen guide,
And turn their crooked Yokes on ev'ry side.
Still as at either End they wheel around,
The Master meets 'em with his Goblet crown'd;
The hearty Draught rewards, renews their Toil;
Then back the turning Plow-shares cleave the Soil:
The new-ear'd Earth in blacker Ridges roll'd;
Sable it look'd, tho' form'd of molten Gold.

Another Field rose high with waving Grain;
With bended Sickles stand the Reaper-Train:

Here stretch'd in Ranks the level'd Swarths are found,
Sheaves heap'd on Sheaves, here thicken up the
    Ground.
With sweeping Stroke the Mowers strow the Lands;
The Gath'rers follow, and collect in Bands;
And last the Children, in whose Arms are born
(Too short to gripe them) the brown Sheaves of Corn.
The rustic Monarch of the Field descries
With silent Glee, the Heaps around him rise.
A ready Banquet on the Turf is laid,
Beneath an ample Oak's expanded Shade.
The Victim-Ox the sturdy Youth prepare;
The Reaper's due Repast, the Women's Care.

  Next, ripe in yellow Gold, a Vineyard shines,
Bent with the pond'rous Harvest of its Vines;
A deeper Dye the dangling Clusters show,
And curl'd on silver Props, in order glow:
A darker Metal mixt, intrench'd the Place;
And Pales of glitt'ring Tin th' Enclosure grace.
To this, one Pathway gently winding leads,
Where march a Train with Baskets on their Heads,
(Fair Maids, and blooming Youths) that smiling
    bear
The purple Product of th' Autumnal Year.
To these a Youth awakes the warbling Strings,
Whose tender Lay the Fate of *Linus* sings;
In measur'd Dance behind him move the Train,
Tune soft the Voice, and answer to the Strain.

  Here, Herds of Oxen march, erect and bold,
Rear high their Horns, and seem to lowe in Gold,
And speed to Meadows on whose sounding Shores
A rapid Torrent thro' the Rushes roars:
Four golden Herdsmen as their Guardians stand,
And nine four Dogs compleat the rustic Band.

Two Lions rushing from the Wood appear'd;
And seiz'd a Bull, the Master of the Herd:
He roar'd: in vain the Dogs, the Men withstood,
They tore his Flesh, and drank the sable Blood.
The Dogs (oft' chear'd in vain) desert the Prey,
Dread the grim Terrors, and at distance bay.

Next this, the Eye the Art of Vulcan leads
Deep thro' fair Forests, and a Length of Meads;
And Stalls, and Folds, and scatter'd Cotts between;
And fleecy Flocks, that whiten all the Scene.

A figur'd Dance succeeds: Such once was seen
In lofty *Gnossus*, for the *Cretan* Queen,
Form'd by *Daedalean* Art. A comely Band
Of Youths and Maidens, bounding Hand in Hand;
The Maids in soft Cymarrs of Linen drest;
The Youths all graceful in the glossy Vest;
Of those the Locks with flow'ry Wreaths inroll'd,
Of these the Sides adorn'd with Swords of Gold,
That glitt'ring gay, from silver Belts depend.
Now all at once they rise, at once descend,
With well-taught Feet: Now shape, in oblique ways,
Confus'dly regular, the moving Maze:
Now forth at once, too swift for sight, they spring,
And undistinguish'd blend the flying Ring:
So whirls a Wheel, in giddy Circle tost,
And rapid as it runs, the single Spokes are lost.
The gazing Multitudes admire around;
Two active Tumblers in the Center bound;
Now high, now low, their pliant Limbs they bend,
And gen'ral Songs the sprightly Revel end.

Thus the broad Shield complete the Artist crown'd
With his last Hand, and pour'd the Ocean round:
In living Silver seem'd the Waves to roll,
And beat the Buckler's Verge, and bound the whole.

THE ODYSSEY

Ulysses and His Dog

THUS, near the gates conferring as they drew,
Argus, the Dog, his ancient master knew;
He, not unconscious of the voice, and tread,
Lifts to the sound his ear, and rears his head.
Bred by *Ulysses*, nourish'd at his board,
But ah! not fated long to please his Lord!
To him, his swiftness and his strength were vain;
The voice of Glory call'd him o'er the main.
'Till then in ev'ry sylvan chace renown'd,
With '*Argus*, *Argus*', rung the woods around;
With him the youth pursu'd the goat or fawn,
Or trac'd the mazy leveret o'er the lawn.
Now left to man's ingratitude he lay,
Un-hous'd, neglected, in the publick way;
And where on heaps the rich manure was spread,
Obscene with reptile, took his sordid bed.

He knew his Lord; he knew, and strove to meet,
In vain he strove, to crawl, and kiss his feet;
Yet (all he could) his tail, his ears, his eyes
Salute his master, and confess his joys.
Soft pity touch'd the mighty master's soul;
Adown his cheek a tear unbidden stole,
Stole unperceiv'd; he turn'd his head, and dry'd
The drop humane: then thus impassion'd cry'd.

'What noble beast in this abandon'd state
Lies here all helpless at *Ulysses*' gate?
His bulk and beauty speak no vulgar praise;
If, as he seems, he was, in better days,

Some care his Age deserves: Or was he priz'd
For worthless beauty? therefore now despis'd?
Such dogs, and men there are, meer things of state,
And always cherish'd by their friends, the Great.'
   'Not *Argus* so' (*Eumaeus* thus rejoin'd)
'But serv'd a master of a nobler kind,
Who never, never shall behold him more!
Long, long since perish'd on a distant shore!
Oh had you seen him, vig'rous, bold and young,
Swift as a stag, and as a lion strong,
Him no fell Savage on the plain withstood,
None 'scap'd him, bosom'd in the gloomy wood;
His eye how piercing, and his scent how true,
To winde the vapour in the tainted dew?
Such, when *Ulysses* left his natal coast;
Now years un-nerve him, and his lord is lost!
The women keep the gen'rous creature bare,
A sleek and idle race is all their care.
The master gone, the servants what restrains?
Or dwells humanity where riot reigns?
Jove fix'd it certain, that whatever day
Makes man a slave, takes half his worth away.'
   This said, the honest herdsman strode before:
The musing Monarch pauses at the door:
The Dog whom Fate had granted to behold
His Lord, when twenty tedious years had roll'd,
Takes a last look, and having seen him, dies;
So clos'd for ever faithful *Argus*' eyes!

THE DUNCIAD

The Triumph of Dulness

O Muse! relate (for you can tell alone,
Wits have short Memories, and Dunces none)
Relate, who first, who last resign'd to rest;
Whose Heads she partly, whose completely bless'd;
What Charms could Faction, what Ambition, lull,
The Venal quiet, and entrance the Dull;
'Till drown'd was Sense, and Shame, and Right, and
    Wrong –
O sing, and hush the Nations with thy Song!

*

In vain, in vain, – the all-composing Hour
Resistless falls: the Muse obeys the Pow'r.
She comes! she comes! the sable Throne behold
Of *Night* Primeval, and of *Chaos* old!
Before her, *Fancy's* gilded clouds decay,
And all its varying Rain-bows die away.
Wit shoots in vain its momentary fires,
The meteor drops, and in a flash expires.
As one by one, at dread Medea's strain,
The sick'ning stars fade off th' ethereal plain;
As Argus' eyes, by Hermes' wand opprest,
Clos'd one by one to everlasting rest;
Thus at her felt approach, and secret might,
Art after *Art* goes out, and all is Night.
See skulking *Truth* to her old cavern fled,
Mountains of Casuistry heap'd o'er her head!

Philosophy, that lean'd on Heav'n before,
Shrinks to her second cause, and is no more.
Physic of *Metaphysic* begs defence,
And *Metaphysic* calls for aid on *Sense*!
See *Mystery* to *Mathematics* fly!
In vain! they gaze, turn giddy, rave, and die.
Religion blushing veils her sacred fires,
And unawares *Morality* expires.
Nor *public* Flame, nor *private*, dares to shine;
Nor *human* Spark is left, nor Glimpse *divine*!
Lo! thy dread Empire, CHAOS! is restor'd;
Light dies before thy uncreating word:
Thy hand, great Anarch! lets the curtain fall;
And universal Darkness buries All.

AN ESSAY ON MAN

ADDRESSED TO HENRY ST JOHN,
LORD BOLINGBROKE[1]

I. Proem

AWAKE, my ST JOHN! leave all meaner things
To low ambition, and the pride of Kings.
Let us (since Life can little more supply
Than just to look about us and to die)
Expatiate free o'er all this scene of Man;
A mighty maze! but not without a plan;
A Wild, where weeds and flow'rs promiscuous shoot;
Or Garden, tempting with forbidden fruit.
Together let us beat this ample field,
Try what the open, what the covert yield;
The latent tracts, the giddy heights, explore
Of all who blindly creep, or sightless soar;
Eye Nature's walks, shoot Folly as it flies,
And catch the Manners living as they rise;
Laugh where we must, be candid where we can;
But vindicate the ways of God to Man.

II. Hope Eternal

HEAV'N from all creatures hides the book of Fate,
All but the page prescrib'd, their present state:
From brutes what men, from men what spirits
    know:
Or who could suffer Being here below?

1. Viscount Bolingbroke (1678–1751); statesman and philosopher.

119

The lamb thy riot dooms to bleed to-day,
Had he thy Reason, would he skip and play?
Pleas'd to the last, he crops the flow'ry food,
And licks the hand just rais'd to shed his blood.
Oh blindness to the future! kindly giv'n,
That each may fill the circle mark'd by Heav'n:
Who sees with equal eye, as God of all,
A hero perish, or a sparrow fall,
Atoms or systems into ruin hurl'd,
And now a bubble burst, and now a world.

Hope humbly then; with trembling pinions soar;
Wait the great teacher Death; and God adore.
What future bliss, he gives not thee to know,
But gives that Hope to be thy blessing now.
Hope springs eternal in the human breast:
Man never Is, but always To be blest:
The soul uneasy, and confin'd from home,
Rests and expatiates in a life to come.

Lo, the poor Indian! whose untutor'd mind
Sees God in clouds, or hears him in the wind;
His soul, proud Science never taught to stray
Far as the solar walk, or milky way;
Yet simple Nature to his hope has giv'n,
Behind the cloud-topt hill, an humbler heav'n;
Some safer world in depth of woods embrac'd,
Some happier island in the wat'ry waste,
Where slaves once more their native land behold,
No fiends torment, no Christians thirst for gold.
To Be, contents his natural desire,
He asks no Angel's wing, no Seraph's fire;
But thinks, admitted to that equal sky,
His faithful dog shall bear him company.

III. The Proper Study

KNOW then thyself, presume not God to scan,
The proper study of Mankind is Man.
Plac'd on this isthmus of a middle state,
A Being darkly wise, and rudely great:
With too much knowledge for the Sceptic side,
With too much weakness for the Stoic's pride,
He hangs between; in doubt to act, or rest;
In doubt to deem himself a God, or Beast;
In doubt his Mind or Body to prefer;
Born but to die, and reas'ning but to err;
Alike in ignorance, his reason such,
Whether he thinks too little, or too much:
Chaos of Thought and Passion, all confus'd;
Still by himself abus'd, or disabus'd;
Created half to rise, and half to fall;
Great Lord of all things, yet a prey to all;
Sole judge of Truth, in endless Error hurl'd:
The glory, jest, and riddle of the world!
   Go, wond'rous creature! mount where Science
     guides,
Go, measure earth, weigh air, and state the tides;
Instruct the planets in what orbs to run,
Correct old Time, and regulate the Sun;
Go, soar with Plato to th' empyreal sphere,
To the first good, first perfect, and first fair;
Or tread the mazy round his follow'rs trod,
And quitting sense call imitating God;
As Eastern priests in giddy circles run,
And turn their heads to imitate the Sun.
Go, teach Eternal Wisdom how to rule --
Then drop into thyself, and be a fool!

Superior beings, when of late they saw
A mortal Man unfold all Nature's law,
Admir'd such wisdom in an earthly shape,
And show'd a NEWTON as we show an ape.

Could he, whose rules the rapid Comet bind,
Describe or fix one movement of his Mind?
Who saw its fires here rise, and there descend,
Explain his own beginning, or his end?
Alas, what wonder! Man's superior part
Uncheck'd may rise, and climb from art to art;
But when his own great work is but begun,
What Reason weaves, by Passion is undone.

Trace Science, then, with Modesty thy guide;
First strip off all her equipage of Pride;
Deduct what is but Vanity, or Dress,
Or Learning's Luxury, or Idleness;
Or tricks to show the stretch of human brain,
Mere curious pleasure, or ingenious pain;
Expunge the whole, or lop th' excrescent parts
Of all our Vices have created Arts;
Then see how little the remaining sum,
Which serv'd the past, and must the times to come!

IV. Opinion's Varying Rays

WHATE'ER the Passion, knowledge, fame, or pelf,
Not one will change his neighbour with himself.
The learn'd is happy nature to explore;
The fool is happy that he knows no more;
The rich is happy in the plenty giv'n,
The poor contents him with the care of Heav'n.
See the blind beggar dance, the cripple sing,
The sot a hero, lunatic a king;

The starving chemist in his golden views
Supremely bless'd, the poet in his Muse.

   See some strange comfort ev'ry state attend.
And pride bestow'd on all, a common friend;
See some fit Passion ev'ry age supply,
Hope travels through, nor quits us when we die.

   Behold the child, by Nature's kindly law,
Pleas'd with a rattle, tickled with a straw:
Some livelier play-thing gives his youth delight,
A little louder, but as empty quite:
Scarfs, garters, gold, amuse his riper stage,
And beads and pray'r-books are the toys of age:
Pleas'd with this bauble still, as that before;
Till tir'd he sleeps, and Life's poor play is o'er.

   Mean-while Opinion gilds with varying rays
Those painted clouds that beautify our days;
Each want of happiness by Hope supply'd,
And each vacuity of sense by Pride:
These build as fast as knowledge can destroy;
In Folly's cup still laughs the bubble, joy;
One prospect lost, another still we gain;
And not a vanity is giv'n in vain;
Ev'n mean Self-love becomes, by force divine,
The scale to measure others wants by thine.
See! and confess, one comfort still must rise,
'Tis this, Tho' Man's a fool, yet GOD IS WISE.

V. Happiness

OH Happiness! our being's end and aim!
Good, Pleasure, Ease, Content! whate'er thy name:
That something still which prompts th' eternal sigh,
For which we bear to live, or dare to die,

Which still so near us, yet beyond us lies,
O'erlook'd, seen double, by the fool, and wise.
Plant of celestial seed! if dropt below,
Say, in what mortal soil thou deign'st to grow?
Fair op'ning to some Court's propitious shine,
Or deep with di'monds in the flaming mine?
Twin'd with the wreaths Parnassian laurels yield,
Or reap'd in iron harvests of the field?
Where grows? -- where grows it not? If vain our toil,
We ought to blame the culture, not the soil:
Fix'd to no spot is Happiness sincere,
'Tis nowhere to be found, or every where;
'Tis never to be bought, but always free,
And, fled from Monarchs, St John! dwells with thee.

VI. Calm Sunshine or Shame

What nothing earthly gives, or can destroy,
The soul's calm sun-shine, and the heart-felt joy,
Is Virtue's prize: A better would you fix?
Then give Humility a coach and six,
Justice a Conqu'ror's sword, or Truth a gown,
Or Public Spirit its great cure, a Crown.
Weak, foolish man! will Heav'n reward us there
With the same trash mad mortals wish for here?
The Boy and Man an individual makes,
Yet sigh'st thou now for apples and for cakes?
Go, like the Indian, in another life
Expect thy dog, thy bottle, and thy wife;
As well as dream such trifles are assign'd,
As toys and empires, for a god-like mind.
Rewards, that either would to Virtue bring
No joy, or be destructive of the thing;

How oft by these at sixty are undone
The virtues of a saint at twenty-one!
To whom can Riches give Repute, or Trust,
Content, or Pleasure, but the Good and Just?
Judges and Senates have been bought for gold,
Esteem and Love were never to be sold.
Oh fool! to think God hates the worthy mind,
The lover and the love of human-kind,
Whose life is healthful, and whose conscience clear,
Because he wants a thousand pounds a year.

Honour and shame from no Condition rise;
Act well your part, there all the honour lies.
Fortune in Men has some small diff'rence made –
One flaunts in rags, one flutters in brocade;
The cobler apron'd, and the parson gown'd,
The friar hooded, and the monarch crown'd.
'What differ more' (you cry) 'than crown and cowl?'
I'll tell you, friend! a wise man and a fool.
You'll find, if once the monarch acts the monk,
Or, cobler-like, the parson will be drunk,
Worth makes the man, and want of it the fellow;
The rest is all but leather or prunella.

Stuck o'er with titles, and hung round with strings,
That thou may'st be by kings, or whores of kings,
Boast the pure blood of an illustrious race,
In quiet flow from Lucrece to Lucrece:
But by your fathers' worth if your's you rate,
Count me those only who were good and great.
Go! if your ancient but ignoble blood
Has crept through scoundrels ever since the flood,
Go! and pretend your family is young;
Nor own, your fathers have been fools so long.
What can ennoble sots, or slaves, or cowards?
Alas! not all the blood of all the HOWARDS.

Look next on Greatness; say where Greatness lies?
'Where, but among the Heroes and the Wise?'
Heroes are much the same, the point's agreed,
From Macedonia's madman to the Swede;[1]
The whole strange purpose of their lives to find
Or make an enemy of all mankind!
Not one looks backward, onward still he goes,
Yet ne'er looks forward farther than his nose.
No less alike the Politic and Wise;
All sly slow things, with circumspective eyes:
Men in their loose unguarded hours they take,
Not that themselves are wise, but others weak.
But grant that those can conquer, these can cheat;
'Tis phrase absurd to call a Villain Great:
Who wickedly is wise, or madly brave,
Is but the more a fool, the more a knave.
Who noble ends by noble means obtains,
Or failing, smiles in exile or in chains,
Like good Aurelius let him reign, or bleed
Like Socrates, that Man is great indeed.

What's Fame? A fancied life in others' breath,
A thing beyond us, ev'n before our death.
Just what you hear, you have, and what's unknown
The same (my Lord) if Tully's, or your own.
All that we feel of it begins and ends
In the small circle of our foes or friends;
To all beside as much an empty shade
An Eugene[2] living, as a Caesar dead;
Alike or when, or where, they shone, or shine,
Or on the Rubicon, or on the Rhine.
A Wit's a feather, and a Chief a rod;
An honest Man's the noblest work of God.

1. Alexander the Great, and Charles XII of Sweden.
2. Prince Eugene of Savoy (1663–1736).

Fame but from death a villain's name can save,
As Justice tears his body from the grave,
When what t' oblivion better were resign'd,
Is hung on high, to poison half mankind.
All fame is foreign, but of true desert;
Plays round the head, but comes not to the heart:
One self-approving hour whole years out-weighs
Of stupid starers, and of loud huzzas;
And more true joy Marcellus[1] exil'd feels,
Than Caesar with a senate at his heels.

   In Parts superior what advantage lies?
Tell (for You can) what is it to be wise?
'Tis but to know how little can be known;
To see all others' faults, and feel our own:
Condemn'd in business or in arts to drudge,
Without a second, or without a judge.
Truths would you teach, or save a sinking land?
All fear, none aid you, and few understand.
Painful pre-eminence! yourself to view
Above life's weakness, and its comforts too.

   Bring then these blessings to a strict account;
Make fair deductions; see to what they mount:
How much of other each is sure to cost;
How each for other oft is wholly lost;
How inconsistent greater goods with these;
How sometimes life is risqu'd, and always ease:
Think, and if still the things thy envy call,
Say, would'st thou be the Man to whom they fall?
To sigh for ribands if you art so silly,
Mark how they grace Lord Umbra, or Sir Billy:
Is yellow dirt the passion of thy life?
Look but on Gripus, or on Gripus' wife:

---

1. An opponent of Caesar.

If Parts allure thee, think how Bacon shined,
The wisest, brightest, meanest of mankind:
Or, ravish'd with the whistling of a Name,
See Cromwell, damn'd to everlasting fame!
If all, united, thy ambition call,
From ancient story learn to scorn them all.
There, in the rich, the honour'd, fam'd, and great,
See the false scale of happiness complete!
In hearts of Kings, or arms of Queens who lay,
How happy! those to ruin, these betray.
Mark by what wretched steps their glory grows,
From dirt and sea-weed as proud Venice rose;
In each how guilt and greatness equal ran,
And all that raised the Hero, sunk the Man:
Now Europe's laurels on their brows behold,
But stain'd with blood, or ill exchang'd for gold:
Then see them broke with toils, or sunk in ease,
Or infamous for plunder'd provinces.
Oh wealth ill-fated! which no act of fame
E'er taught to shine, or sanctify'd from shame!
What greater bliss attends their close of life?
Some greedy minion, or imperious wife,
The trophy'd arches, story'd halls invade,
And haunt their slumbers in the pompous shade.
Alas! not dazzled with their noontide ray,
Compute the morn and ev'ning to the day;
The whole amount of that enormous fame,
A Tale, that blends their glory with their shame!

VII. Epilogue

COME then, my Friend, my Genius! come along;
O master of the poet, and the song!
And while the Muse now stoops, or now ascends,
To Man's low passions, or their glorious ends,
Teach me, like thee, in various nature wise,
To fall with dignity, with temper rise;
Form'd by thy converse, happily to steer
From grave to gay, from lively to severe;
Correct with spirit, eloquent with ease,
Intent to reason, or polite to please.
Oh! while along the stream of Time thy name
Expanded flies, and gathers all its fame,
Say, shall my little bark attendant sail,
Pursue the triumph, and partake the gale?
When statesmen, heroes, kings, in dust repose,
Whose sons shall blush their fathers were thy foes,
Shall then this verse to future age pretend
Thou wert my guide, philosopher, and friend?
That, urg'd by thee, I turn'd the tuneful art
From sounds to things, from fancy to the heart;
For Wit's false mirror held up Nature's light;
Show'd erring Pride, WHATEVER IS, IS RIGHT;
That REASON, PASSION, answer one great aim;
That true SELF-LOVE and SOCIAL are the same;
That VIRTUE only makes our Bliss below;
And all our Knowledge is, OURSELVES TO KNOW.

MORAL ESSAYS

EPISTLE I

TO

SIR RICHARD TEMPLE, LORD COBHAM[1]

Of the Knowledge and Characters

of MEN

I

YES, you despise the man to Books confin'd,
Who from his study rails at human kind;
Tho' what he learns he speaks, and may advance
Some gen'ral maxims, or be right by chance.
The coxcomb bird, so talkative and grave,
That from his cage cries Cuckold, Whore, and Knave,
Tho' many a passenger he rightly call,
You hold him no Philosopher at all.

And yet the fate of all extremes is such,
Men may be read, as well as Books, too much.
To observations which ourselves we make,
We grow more partial for th' Observer's sake;
To written Wisdom, as another's, less:
Maxims are drawn from Notions, those from Guess.
There's some Peculiar in each leaf and grain,
Some unmark'd fibre, or some varying vein:
Shall only Man be taken in the gross?
Grant but as many sorts of Mind as Moss.[2]

That each from other differs, first confess;
Next, that he varies from himself no less:
Add Nature's, Custom's, Reason's, Passion's strife,
And all Opinion's colours cast on life.

1. Viscount Cobham (1669–1749); general, politician and friend of
   Pope's.
2. There are above 300 sorts of moss observed by naturalists. *P.*

Our depths who fathoms, or our shallows finds,
Quick whirls, and shifting eddies, of our minds?
On human Actions reason though you can,
It may be Reason, but it is not Man:
His Principle of action once explore,
That instant 'tis his Principle no more.
Like following life through creatures you dissect,
You lose it in the moment you detect.

Yet more; the diff'rence is as great between
The optics seeing, as the objects seen.
All Manners take a tincture from our own;
Or come discolour'd, through our Passions shown;
Or Fancy's beam enlarges, multiplies,
Contracts, inverts, and gives ten thousand dyes.

Nor will Life's stream for Observation stay,
It hurries all too fast to mark their way:
In vain sedate reflections we would make,
When half our knowledge we must snatch, not take.
Oft, in the Passions' wild rotation toss'd,
Our spring of action to ourselves is lost:
Tir'd, not determin'd, to the last we yield,
And what comes then is master of the field.
As the last image of that troubled heap,
When Sense subsides, and Fancy sports in sleep,
(Tho' past the recollection of the thought),
Becomes the stuff of which our dream is wrought:
Something as dim to our internal view,
Is thus, perhaps, the cause of most we do.

True, some are open, and to all men known;
Others so very close they're hid from none;
(So Darkness strikes the sense no less than Light)
Thus gracious CHANDOS[1] is belov'd at sight;

1. James Brydges, Duke of Chandos (1673–1744).

And ev'ry child hates Shylock, tho' his soul
Still sits at squat, and peeps not from its hole.
At half mankind when gen'rous Manly[1] raves,
All know 'tis Virtue, for he thinks them knaves:
When universal homage Umbra pays,
All see 'tis Vice, and itch of vulgar praise.
When Flatt'ry glares, all hate it in a Queen,
While one there is who charms us with his Spleen.

But these plain Characters we rarely find;
Tho' strong the bent, yet quick the turns of mind:
Or puzzling Contraries confound the whole;
Or Affectations quite reverse the soul.
The Dull, flat Falsehood serves for policy;
And, in the Cunning, Truth itself's a lie:
Unthought-of Frailties cheat us in the Wise;
The Fool lies hid in inconsistencies.

See the same man, in vigour, in the gout;
Alone, in company; in place, or out;
Early at Bus'ness, and at Hazard late;
Mad at a Fox-chace, wise at a Debate;
Drunk at a Borough, civil at a Ball;
Friendly at Hackney, faithless at Whitehall.

Catius is ever moral, ever grave,
Thinks who endures a knave, is next a knave,
Save just at dinner – then prefers, no doubt,
A Rogue with Ven'son to a Saint without.

Who would not praise Patritio's high desert,
His hand unstain'd, his uncorrupted heart,
His comprehensive head! all Int'rests weigh'd,
All Europe sav'd, yet Britain not betray'd?
He thanks you not, his pride is in Picquette,
New-market fame, and judgment at a Bet.

1. Character in Wycherley's comedy of the *Plain Dealer*.

What made (say Montaigne, or more sage
    Charron[1])
Otho a warrior, Cromwell a buffoon?
A perjur'd Prince a leaden Saint revere,[2]
A godless Regent tremble at a Star?[3]
The throne a Bigot keep, a Genius quit,
Faithless through Piety, and dup'd through Wit?[4]
Europe a Woman, Child, or Dotard rule,
And just her wisest monarch made a fool?

Know, GOD and NATURE only are the same:
In Man, the judgment shoots at flying game;
A bird of passage! gone as soon as found,
Now in the Moon perhaps, now under ground.

II

In vain the Sage, with retrospective eye,
Would from th' apparent What conclude the Why,
Infer the Motive from the Deed, and shew
That what we chanc'd was what we meant to do.
Behold! if Fortune or a Mistress frowns,
Some plunge in bus'ness, others shave their crowns:
To ease the Soul of one oppressive weight,
This quits an Empire, that embroils a State:

1. An imitator of Montaigne.
2. Louis XI of France wore in his hat a leaden image of the Virgin
Mary, which when he swore by he feared to break his oath. *P.*
3. Philip, Duke of Orleans, Regent in the minority of Louis XV,
superstitious in judicial astrology, though an unbeliever in all
religion. *P.*
4. Philip V of Spain, who, after renouncing the throne for religion,
resumed it to gratify his queen; and Victor Amadeus II, King of
Sardinia, who resigned the crown, and, trying to re-assume it, was
imprisoned till his death. *P.*

The same adust complexion has impell'd
Charles to the Convent, Philip to the Field.[1]
  Not always Actions show the man: we find
Who does a kindness, is not therefore kind;
Perhaps Prosperity becalm'd his breast,
Perhaps the Wind just shifted from the east:
Not therefore humble he who seeks retreat,
Pride guides his steps, and bids him shun the
    great:
Who combats bravely is not therefore brave,
He dreads a death-bed like the meanest slave:
Who reasons wisely is not therefore wise,
His pride in Reas'ning, not in acting Lies.
  But grant that Actions best discover man;
Take the most strong, and sort them as you can:
The few that glare each character must mark,
You balance not the many in the dark.
What will you do with such as disagree?
Suppress them, or miscall them Policy?
Must then at once (the character to save)
The plain rough Hero turn a crafty Knave?
Alas! in truth the man but chang'd his mind,
Perhaps was sick, in love, or had not din'd.
Ask why from Britain Caesar would retreat?
Caesar himself might whisper he was beat.
Why risk the world's great empire for a Punk?
Caesar perhaps might answer he was drunk.
But, sage historians! 'tis your task to prove
One action, Conduct; one, heroic Love.
  'Tis from high Life high Characters are drawn;
A Saint in Crape is twice a Saint in Lawn;
A Judge is just, a Chanc'lor juster still;
A Gownman, learn'd; a Bishop, what you will;

1. Charles V and Philip II of Spain.

Wise, if a Minister; but, if a King,
More wise, more learn'd, more just, more ev'ry
    thing.
Court-Virtues bear, like Gems, the highest rate,
Born where Heav'n's influence scarce can penetrate:
In life's low vale, the soil the Virtues like,
They please as beauties, here as wonders strike.
Tho' the same Sun with all-diffusive rays
Blush in the Rose, and in the Di'mond blaze,
We prize the stronger effort of his pow'r,
And justly set the Gem above the Flow'r.

    'Tis Education forms the common mind,
Just as the Twig is bent, the Tree's inclin'd.
Boastful and rough, your first son is a 'Squire;
The next a Tradesman, meek, and much a liar;
Tom struts a Soldier, open, bold, and brave;
Will sneaks a Scriv'ner, an exceeding knave:
Is he a Churchman? then he's fond of pow'r: ⎫
A Quaker? sly: A Presbyterian? sour: ⎬
A smart Free-thinker? all things in an hour. ⎭

    Ask men's Opinions: Scoto now shall tell
How Trade increases, and the World goes well;
Strike off his Pension, by the setting sun,
And Britain, if not Europe, is undone.

    That gay Free-thinker, a fine talker once,
What turns him now a stupid silent dunce?
Some God, or Spirit he has lately found;
Or chanc'd to meet a Minister that frown'd.

    Judge we by Nature? Habit can efface,
Int'rest o'ercome, or Policy take place:
By Actions? those Uncertainty divides:
By Passions? these Dissimulation hides:
Opinions? they still take a wider range:
Find, if you can, in what you cannot change.

Manners with Fortunes, Humours turn with
　Climes,
Tenets with Books, and Principles with Times.

III

Search, then, the RULING PASSION: There, alone,
The Wild are constant, and the Cunning known;
The Fool consistent, and the False sincere;
Priests, Princes, Women, no dissemblers here.
This clue once found, unravels all the rest,
The prospect clears, and WHARTON stands confess'd.[1]
Wharton, the scorn and wonder of our days,
Whose Ruling Passion was the Lust of Praise:
Born with whate'er could win it from the Wise,
Women and Fools must like him or he dies;
Tho' wondering Senates hung on all he spoke,
The Club must hail him master of the joke.
Shall parts so various aim at nothing new?
He'll shine a Tully and a Wilmot[2] too.
Then turns repentant, and his God adores
With the same spirit that he drinks and whores;
Enough, if all around him but admire,
And now the Punk applaud, and now the Friar.
Thus with each gift of nature and of art,
And wanting nothing but an honest heart;
Grown all to all, from no one Vice exempt;
And most contemptible, to shun contempt;

1. Philip Wharton, Duke of Wharton (1698–1731); statesman and
　brilliant orator; outlawed for Jacobitism, 1729.
2. John Wilmot, Earl of Rochester, famous for his wit and extrava-
　gances in the time of Charles II. *P.*

His Passion still to covet gen'ral praise,
His Life, to forfeit it a thousand ways;
A constant Bounty which no friend has made;
An angel Tongue, which no man can persuade;
A Fool, with more of Wit than half mankind,
Too rash for Thought, for Action too refin'd;
A Tyrant to the wife his heart approves;
A Rebel to the very king he loves;
He dies, sad out-cast of each church and state,
And, harder still! flagitious, yet not great.
Ask you why Wharton broke through ev'ry rule?
'Twas all for fear the Knaves should call him Fool.

    Nature well known, no prodigies remain,
Comets are regular, and WHARTON plain.

    Yet, in this search, the wisest may mistake,
If second qualities for first they take.
When Catiline by rapine swell'd his store;
When Caesar made a noble dame a whore;
In this the Lust, in that the Avarice
Were means, not ends; Ambition was the vice.
That very Caesar, born in Scipio's days,
Had aim'd, like him, by Chastity at praise.
Lucullus, when Frugality could charm,
Had roasted turnips in the Sabin farm.
In vain th' observer eyes the builder's toil,
But quite mistakes the scaffold for the pile.

    In this one Passion man can strength enjoy,
As Fits give vigour, just when they destroy.
Time, that on all things lays his lenient hand,
Yet tames not this; it sticks to our last sand.
Consistent in our follies and our sins,
Here honest Nature ends as she begins.

    Old Politicians chew on wisdom past,
And totter on in bus'ness to the last;

As weak, as earnest, and as gravely out,
As sober Lanesb'row dancing in the gout.[1]

Behold a rev'rend sire, whom want of grace
Has made the father of a nameless race,
Shov'd from the wall perhaps, or rudely press'd
By his own son, that passes by unbless'd:
Still to his wench he crawls on knocking knees,
And envies ev'ry sparrow that he sees.

A salmon's belly, Helluo, was thy fate;
The doctor call'd, declares all help too late:
'Mercy!' cries Helluo, 'mercy on my soul!
Is there no hope? – Alas! – then bring the jowl.'

The frugal Crone, whom praying priests attend,
Still tries to save the hallow'd taper's end,
Collects her breath, as ebbing life retires,
For one puff more, and in that puff expires.

'Odious! in woollen! 'twould a Saint provoke,'
(Were the last words that poor Narcissa[2] spoke),
'No, let a charming Chintz and Brussels lace
Wrap my cold limbs, and shade my lifeless face:
One would not, sure, be frightful when one's dead –
And – Betty – give this Cheek a little Red.'

The Courtier smooth, who forty years had shin'd
An humble servant to all human kind,
Just brought out this, when scarce his tongue could
        stir,
'If – where I'm going – I could serve you, Sir?'

1. An ancient nobleman, who continued this practice long after his legs were disabled by the gout. Upon the death of Prince George of Denmark, he demanded an audience of the Queen, to advise her to preserve her health and dispel her grief by dancing. *P.*
2. ... Several attribute this to a very celebrated actress, who in detestation of the thought of being buried in woollen, gave these last orders with her dying breath. *P.* An act of 1678 to protect the woollen industry obliged the dead to be buried in woollen.

'I give and I devise' (old Euclio said,
And sigh'd) 'my lands and tenements to Ned.'
'Your money, Sir?' 'My money, Sir, what all?
Why – if I must' – (then wept) 'I give it Paul.'
'The Manor, Sir?' – 'The Manor! hold' (he cried),
'Not that, – I cannot part with that' – and died.

And you, brave COBHAM! to the latest breath
Shall feel your ruling passion strong in death:
Such in those moments as in all the past,
'Oh, save my Country, Heav'n!' shall be your last.

EPISTLE II

TO A LADY[1]

Of the Characters of WOMEN

NOTHING so true as what you once let fall,
'Most Women have no Characters at all.'
Matter too soft a lasting mark to bear,
And best distinguish'd by black, brown, or fair.

How many pictures of one Nymph we view,
All how unlike each other, all how true!
Arcadia's Countess, here, in ermin'd pride,
Is there, Pastora by a fountain side.
Here Fannia, leering on her own good man,
And there, a naked Leda with a Swan.
Let then the Fair one beautifully cry,
In Magdalen's loose hair and lifted eye,
Or dress'd in smiles of sweet Cecilia shine,
With simp'ring Angels, Palms, and Harps divine;
Whether the Charmer sinner it or saint it,
If Folly grow romantic, I must paint it.

1. Martha Blount, see p. 81, n. 1.

Come then, the colours and the ground prepare!
Dip in the Rainbow, trick her off in Air;
Choose a firm Cloud, before it fall, and in it
Catch, e'er she change, the Cynthia of this minute.

Rufa, whose eye quick-glancing o'er the Park,
Attracts each light gay meteor of a Spark,
Agrees as ill with Rufa studying Locke,
As Sappho's di'monds with her dirty smock;
Or Sappho at her toilet's greasy task,
With Sappho fragrant at an ev'ning Mask:
So morning Insects that in muck begun,
Shine, buzz, and fly-blow in the setting sun.

How soft is Silia! fearful to offend;
The frail one's advocate, the weak one's friend:
To her, Calista prov'd her conduct nice;
And good Simplicius asks of her advice.
Sudden, she storms! she raves! You tip the wink,
But spare your censure; Silia does not drink.
All eyes may see from what the change arose,
All eyes may see – a Pimple on her nose.

Papillia, wedded to her am'rous spark,
Sighs for the shades! – 'How charming is a Park!'
A Park is purchas'd, but the Fair he sees
All bath'd in tears – 'Oh odious, odious Trees!'

Ladies, like variegated Tulips, show,
'Tis to their Changes half their charms we owe;
Fine by defect, and delicately weak,
Their happy Spots the nice admirer take.
'Twas thus Calypso once each heart alarm'd,
Aw'd without Virtue, without Beauty charm'd;
Her Tongue bewitch'd as oddly as her Eyes,
Less Wit than Mimic, more a Wit than wise;
Strange graces still, and stranger flights she had,
Was just not ugly, and was just not mad;

Yet ne'er so sure our passion to create,
As when she touch'd the drink of all we hate.
  Narcissa's nature, tolerably mild,
To make a wash, would hardly stew a child;
Has ev'n been prov'd to grant a Lover's pray'r,
And paid a Tradesman once, to make him stare;
Gave alms at Easter, in a Christian trim,
And made a Widow happy, for a whim.
Why then declare Good-nature is her scorn,
When 'tis by that alone she can be born?
Why pique all mortals, yet affect a name?
A fool to Pleasure, yet a slave to Fame:
Now deep in Taylor and the Book of Martyrs,[1]
Now drinking citron with his Grace and Chartres:[2]
Now Conscience chills her, and now Passion burns;
And Atheism and Religion take their turns;
A very Heathen in the carnal part,
Yet still a sad, good Christian at her heart.
  See Sin in State, majestically drunk;
Proud as a Peeress, prouder as a Punk;
Chaste to her Husband, frank to all beside,
A teeming Mistress, but a barren Bride.
What then? let Blood and Body bear the fault,
Her Head's untouch'd, that noble seat of Thought:
Such this day's doctrine – in another fit
She sins with Poets through pure Love of Wit.
What has not fir'd her bosom or her brain –
Caesar and Tall-boy,[3] Charles and Charlema'ne?
As Helluo, late Dictator of the Feast,
The Nose of Haut goût, and the Tip of Taste,

1. Jeremy Taylor's *Holy Living and Holy Dying*, and John Foxe's *Book of Martyrs*.
2. See p. 149, n. 1.
3. Character in a comic opera, *The Jovial Crew*.

Critiqu'd your wine, and analyz'd your meat,
Yet on plain pudding deign'd at home to eat;
So Philomedé, lect'ring all mankind
On the soft Passion and the Taste refin'd,
Th' Address, the Delicacy – stoops at once,
And makes her hearty meal upon a Dunce.

　Flavia's a Wit, has too much sense to pray;
To toast our wants and wishes, is her way;
Nor asks of God, but of her Stars, to give
The mighty blessing, 'While we live, to live.'
Then all for Death, that Opiate of the soul!
Lucretia's dagger, Rosamonda's bowl.
Say, what can cause such impotence of mind?
A Spark too fickle, or a Spouse too kind.
Wise Wretch! with pleasures too refin'd to please;
With too much Spirit to be e'er at ease;
With too much Quickness ever to be taught;
With too much Thinking to have common Thought:
You purchase Pain with all that Joy can give,
And die of nothing, but a Rage to live.

　Turn then from Wits; and look on Simo's Mate,
No Ass so meek, no Ass so obstinate.
Or her, that owns her Faults, but never mends,
Because she's honest, and the best of Friends.
Or her, whose life the Church and Scandal share,
For ever in a Passion or a Pray'r.
Or her, who laughs at Hell, but (like her Grace)
Cries, 'Ah! how charming, if there's no such place!'
Or who in sweet vicissitude appears
Of Mirth and Opium, Ratafie and Tears,
The daily Anodyne, and nightly Draught,
To kill those foes to fair ones, Time and Thought.
Woman and Fool are two hard things to hit;
For true No-meaning puzzles more than Wit.

But what are these to great Atossa's mind?
Scarce once herself, by turns all Womankind!
Who, with herself, or others, from her birth
Finds all her life one warfare upon earth:
Shines, in exposing Knaves, and painting Fools,
Yet is whate'er she hates and ridicules.
No Thought advances, but her Eddy Brain
Whisks it about, and down it goes again.
Full sixty years the World has been her Trade,
The wisest Fool much Time has ever made.
From loveless Youth to unrespected Age
No Passion gratified, except her Rage.
So much the Fury still out-ran the Wit,
The Pleasure miss'd her, and the Scandal hit.
Who breaks with her, provokes Revenge from Hell,
But he's a bolder man who dares be well.
Her ev'ry turn with Violence pursu'd,
Nor more a storm her Hate than Gratitude:
To that each Passion turns, or soon or late;
Love, if it makes her yield, must make her hate:
Superiors? death! and Equals? what a curse!
But an Inferior not dependent? worse!
Offend her, and she knows not to forgive:
Oblige her, and she'll hate you while you live:
But die, and she'll adore you – Then the Bust
And Temple rise – then fall again to dust.
Last night, her Lord was all that's good and great:
A Knave this morning, and his Will a Cheat.
Strange! by the Means defeated of the Ends,
By Spirit robb'd of Pow'r, by Warmth of Friends,
By Wealth of Follow'rs! without one distress,
Sick of herself through very selfishness!
Atossa, curs'd with ev'ry granted pray'r,
Childless with all her Children, wants an Heir.

To Heirs unknown descends th' unguarded store,
Or wanders, Heav'n-directed, to the Poor.
    Pictures like these, dear Madam, to design,
Asks no firm hand, and no unerring line;
Some wand'ring touches, some reflected light,
Some flying stroke alone can hit 'em right:
For how should equal Colours do the knack?
Chameleons who can paint in white and black?
    'Yet Cloe, sure, was form'd without a spot' –
Nature in her then err'd not, but forgot.
'With ev'ry pleasing, ev'ry prudent part,
Say, what can Cloe want?' – She wants a Heart.
She speaks, behaves, and acts just as she ought;
But never, never reach'd one gen'rous Thought.
Virtue she finds too painful an endeavour,
Content to dwell in Decencies for ever.
So very reasonable, so unmov'd,
As never yet to love, or to be lov'd.
She, while her Lover pants upon her breast,
Can mark the figures on an Indian chest;
And when she sees her Friend in deep despair,
Observes how much a Chintz exceeds Mohair.
Forbid it, Heav'n, a Favour or a Debt
She e'er should cancel! – but she may forget.
Safe is your Secret still in Cloe's ear;
But none of Cloe's shall you ever hear.
Of all her Dears she never slander'd one,
But cares not if a thousand are undone.
Would Cloe know if you're alive or dead?
She bids her Footman put it in her head.
Cloe is prudent – Would you, too, be wise?
Then never break your heart when Cloe dies.
    One certain portrait may (I grant) be seen,
Which Heav'n has varnish'd out, and made a *Queen*:

THE SAME FOR EVER! and describ'd by all
With Truth and Goodness, as with Crown and Ball.
Poets heap Virtues, Painters Gems at will,
And show their zeal, and hide their want of skill.
'Tis well – but, Artists! who can paint or write,
To draw the Naked is your true delight.
That Robe of Quality so struts and swells,
None see what Parts of Nature it conceals:
Th' exactest traits of Body or of Mind,
We owe to models of an humble kind,
If QUEENSBERRY[1] to strip there's no compelling,
'Tis from a Handmaid we must take an Helen.
From Peer or Bishop 'tis no easy thing
To draw the man who loves his God, or King:
Alas! I copy (or my draught would fail)
From honest Mah'met,[2] or plain Parson Hale.[3]

But grant, in Public, Men sometimes are shown,
A Woman's seen in Private Life alone:
Our bolder Talents in full light display'd;
Your Virtues open fairest in the shade.
Bred to disguise, in Public 'tis you hide;
There, none distinguish 'twixt your Shame or Pride,
Weakness or Delicacy; all so nice,
That each may seem a Virtue, or a Vice.

In Men, we various Ruling Passions find;
In Women, two almost divide the kind;
Those, only fix'd, they first or last obey,
The Love of Pleasure, and the Love of Sway.

1. Catherine Douglas, Duchess of Queensbery (d. 1777); an eccentric beauty.
2. Servant to the late king, said to be the son of a Turkish Bassa ... *P.*
3. Dr. Stephen Hale, not more estimable for his useful discoveries as a natural philosopher, than for his exemplary life as a parish priest. *P.*

That, Nature gives; and where the lesson taught
Is but to please, can Pleasure seem a fault?
Experience, this; by Man's oppression curst,
They seek the second not to lose the first.

Men, some to Bus'ness, some to Pleasure take;
But ev'ry Woman is at heart a Rake:
Men, some to Quiet, some to public Strife;
But ev'ry Lady would be Queen for life.

Yet mark the fate of a whole sex of Queens!
Pow'r all their end, but Beauty all the means:
In Youth they conquer, with so wild a rage,
As leaves them scarce a subject in their Age:
For foreign glory, foreign joy, they roam;
No thought of peace or happiness at home.
But Wisdom's triumph is well-tim'd Retreat,
As hard a science to the Fair as Great!
Beauties, like Tyrants, old and friendless grown,
Yet hate repose, and dread to be alone,
Worn out in public, weary ev'ry eye,
Nor leave one sigh behind them when they die.

Pleasures the sex, as children Birds, pursue,
Still out of reach, yet never out of view;
Sure, if they catch, to spoil the Toy at most,
To covet flying, and regret when lost:
At last, to follies Youth could scarce defend,
It grows their Age's prudence to pretend;
Asham'd to own they gave delight before,
Reduc'd to feign it, when they give no more:
As Hags hold Sabbaths, less for joy than spight,
So these their merry, miserable Night;
Still round and round the Ghosts of Beauty glide,
And haunt the places where their honour died.

See how the World its Veterans rewards!
A Youth of Frolics, an old Age of Cards;

Fair to no purpose, artful to no end,
Young without Lovers, old without a Friend;
A Fop their Passion, but their Prize a Sot,
Alive, ridiculous; and dead, forgot!

Ah, Friend! to dazzle let the Vain design;
To raise the Thought, and touch the Heart, be thine!
That Charm shall grow, while what fatigues the Ring,
Flaunts and goes down, an unregarded thing:
So when the Sun's broad beam has tir'd the sight,
All mild ascends the Moon's more sober light,
Serene in Virgin Modesty she shines,
And unobserv'd the glaring Orb declines.

Oh! blest with Temper, whose unclouded ray
Can make to-morrow chearful as to-day;
She, who can love a Sister's charms, or hear
Sighs for a Daughter with unwounded ear;
She, who ne'er answers till a Husband cools,
Or, if she rules him, never shows she rules;
Charms by accepting, by submitting sways,
Yet has her humour most, when she obeys;
Let Fops or Fortune fly which way they will;
Disdains all loss of Tickets, or Codille;
Spleen, Vapours, or Small-pox, above them all,
And Mistress of herself, though China fall.

And yet, believe me, good as well as ill,
Woman's at best a Contradiction still.
Heav'n, when it strives to polish all it can
Its last, best work, but forms a softer Man;
Picks from each sex, to make the Fav'rite blest,
Your love of Pleasure, our desire of Rest:
Blends, in exception to all gen'ral rules,
Your Taste of Follies, with our Scorn of Fools:

1. See p. 41, n. 1.

147

Reserve with Frankness, Art with Truth allied,
Courage with Softness, Modesty with Pride;
Fix'd Principles, with Fancy ever new;
Shakes all together, and produces – You.

Be this a Woman's Fame: with this unblest,
Toasts live a scorn, and Queens may die a jest.
This Phoebus promis'd (I forget the year)
When those blue eyes first open'd on the sphere;
Ascendant Phoebus watch'd that hour with care,
Averted half your Parents' simple Prayer;
And gave you Beauty, but deny'd the Pelf
That buys your Sex a Tyrant o'er itself.
The gen'rous God, who Wit and Gold refines,
And ripens Spirits as he ripens Mines,
Kept Dross for Duchesses, the world shall know it,
To you gave Sense, Good-humour, and a Poet.

EPISTLE III

TO ALLEN LORD BATHURST[1]

Of the Use of RICHES

P. WHO shall decide, when Doctors disagree,
And soundest Casuists doubt, like you and me?
You hold the word, from Jove to Momus giv'n,
That Man was made the standing jest of Heav'n:
And Gold but sent to keep the fools in play,
For some to heap, and some to throw away.

But I, who think more highly of our kind,
(And, surely, Heav'n and I are of a mind)
Opine, that Nature, as in duty bound,
Deep hid the shining mischief under ground:

1. Allen Apsley, Lord Bathurst (1684–1775); M.P., and friend of
Pope's.

But when, by Man's audacious labour won,
Flam'd forth this rival to its Sire, the Sun,
Then careful Heav'n supply'd two sorts of Men,
To squander These, and Those to hide agen.

    Like Doctors thus, when much dispute has pass'd,
We find our tenets just the same at last.
Both fairly owning, Riches, in effect,
No grace of Heav'n or token of th' Elect;
Giv'n to the Fool, the Mad, the Vain, the Evil,
To Ward, to Waters, Chartres, and the Devil.[1]

    B. What Nature wants, commodious Gold bestows,
'Tis thus we eat the bread another sows.

    P. But how unequal it bestows, observe,
'Tis thus we riot, while who sow it starve:
What Nature wants (a phrase I much distrust)
Extends to Luxury, extends to Lust:
Useful, I grant, it serves what life requires,
But dreadful too, the dark Assassin hires:

1. John Ward, of Hackney, Esq., member of Parliament, being prosecuted ... and convicted of forgery, was first expelled the House, and then stood in the pillory ... During his confinement, his amusement was to give poison to dogs and cats, and see them expire by slower or quicker torments ... Francis Chartres, a man infamous for all manner of vices. When he was an ensign in the army, he was drummed out of the regiment for a cheat ... After a hundred tricks at the gaming tables, he took to lending money at an exorbitant interest ... in a word, by the constant attention to the vices, wants, and follies of mankind, he acquired an immense fortune. His house was a perpetual bawdy-house. He was twice condemned for rapes, and pardoned ... He died in Scotland, in 1731, aged sixty-two. The populace at his funeral raised a great riot, almost tore the body out of the coffin, and cast dead dogs, etc., into the grave along with it ... Mr Waters, the third of these worthies, was a man no way resembling the former in his military, but extremely so in his civil capacity; his great fortune having been raised by the like attendance on the necessities of others ... *P.*

    B. Trade it may help, Society extend.
    P. But lures the Pirate, and corrupts the Friend.
    B. It raises Armies in a Nation's aid.
    P. But bribes a Senate, and the Land's betray'd.
In vain may Heroes fight, and Patriots rave;
If secret Gold sap on from knave to knave.
Once, we confess, beneath the Patriot's cloak,[1]
From the crack'd bag the dropping Guinea spoke,
And jingling down the back-stairs, told the crew,
'Old Cato is as great a Rogue as you.'
Blest paper-credit! last and best supply!
That lends Corruption lighter wings to fly!
Gold imp'd by thee, can compass hardest things,
Can pocket States, can fetch or carry Kings;
A single leaf shall waft an Army o'er,
Or ship off Senates to a distant shore;[2]
A leaf, like Sibyl's, scatter to and fro
Our fates and fortunes, as the winds shall blow:
Pregnant with thousands flits the Scrap unseen,
And silent sells a King, or buys a Queen,
    Oh! that such Bulky bribes as all might see,
Still, as of old, encumber'd Villainy!
Could France or Rome divert our brave designs,
With all their brandies, or with all their wines?
What could they more than Knights and Squires con-
    found,
Or water all the Quorum ten miles round?

1. This is a true story, which happened in the reign of William III
   to an unsuspected old patriot, who, coming out of the back-door
   from having been closeted by the king, where he had received a
   large bag of guineas, the bursting of the bag discovered his busi-
   ness there. *P.*
2. Alludes to several ministers, councillors, and patriots, banished in
   our time to Siberia, and to that more glorious fate of the Parlia-
   ment of Paris, banished to Pontoise in the year 1720. *P.*

A Statesman's slumbers how this speech would
    spoil!
'Sir, Spain has sent a thousand jars of oil;
Huge bales of British cloth blockade the door;
A hundred oxen at your levée roar.'
    Poor Avarice one torment more would find;
Nor could Profusion squander all in kind.
Astride his cheese, Sir Morgan might we meet;
And Worldly crying coals from street to street,[1]
Whom, with a wig so wild, and mien so maz'd,
Pity mistakes for some poor tradesman craz'd.
Had Colepepper's whole wealth been hops and hogs,
Could he himself have sent it to the dogs?[2]
His Grace will game: to White's[3] a Bull be led,
With spurning heels, and with a butting head:
To White's be carry'd, as to ancient games,
Fair Coursers, Vases, and alluring Dames.
Shall then Uxorio, if the stakes he sweep,
Bear home six Whores and make his Lady weep?
Or soft Adonis, so perfum'd and fine,
Drive to St James's a whole herd of swine?
Oh filthy check on all industrious skill,
To spoil the nation's last great trade, Quadrille!

1. Some misers of great wealth, proprietors of the coal-mines, had
entered at this time into an association to keep up coals to an ex-
travagant price, whereby the poor were reduced almost to starve,
till one of them, taking advantage of underselling the rest, defeated
the design. One of these misers was worth ten thousand, another
seven thousand a year. *P.*

2. Sir William Colepepper, Bart, a person of an ancient family, and
ample fortune, without one other quality of a gentleman, who,
after ruining himself at the gaming-table, passed the rest of his
days in sitting there to see the ruin of others: preferring to subsist
upon borrowing and begging rather than to enter into any reput-
able method of life ... *P.*

3. White's Chocolate House in St James's Street, a haunt of gamblers.

Since then, my Lord, on such a World we fall,
What say you?

    B.   Say! Why, take it, Gold and all.

    P. What Riches give us, let us then inquire:
Meat, Fire, and Clothes.

    B.   What more?

    P.   Meat, Clothes, and Fire.
Is this too little? would you more than live?
Alas! 'tis more than Turner finds they give.[1]
Alas! 'tis more than (all his Visions past)
Unhappy Wharton,[2] waking, found at last!
What can they give? to dying Hopkins, Heirs;[3]
To Chartres, Vigour; Japhet,[4] Nose and Ears?
Can they in gems bid pallid Hippia glow,
In Fulvia's buckle ease the throbs below;
Or heal, old Narses, thy obscener ail,
With all th' embroid'ry plaster'd at thy tail?
They might (were Harpax not too wise to spend)
Give Harpax' self the blessing of a Friend;
Or find some Doctor that would save the life
Of wretched Shylock, spite of Shylock's Wife:
But thousands die, without or this or that,
Die, and endow a College, or a Cat.[5]
To some, indeed, Heav'n grants the happier fate,
T' enrich a Bastard, or a Son they hate.

    Perhaps you think the Poor might have their part?
Bond damns the Poor, and hates them from his heart:[6]

1. Richard Turner, a notorious miser.   2. See p. 136, n. 1.
3. A citizen, whose rapacity obtained him the name of Vulture ... *P*.
4. Japhet Crooke ... who was punished with the loss of those parts,
for having forged a conveyance of an estate to himself ... *P*.
5. A famous Duchess ... in her last will, left considerable legacies and
annuities to her cats. *P*.
6. Dennis Bond, M.P., expelled the House of Commons for a breach
of trust.

The grave Sir Gilbert holds it for a rule,
That 'ev'ry man in want is knave or fool:'[1]
'God cannot love' (says Blunt, with tearless eyes)[2]
'The wretch he starves' – and piously denies:
But the good Bishop, with a meeker air,
Admits, and leaves them, Providence's care.

    Yet, to be just to these poor men of pelf,
Each does but hate his neighbour as himself:
Damn'd to the Mines, an equal fate betides
The Slave that digs it, and the Slave that hides.

    B. Who suffer thus, mere charity should own,
Must act on motives pow'rful, tho' unknown.

    P. Some War, some Plague, or Famine they fore-
see,
Some Revelation hid from you and me.
Why Shylock wants a meal, the cause is found,
He thinks a Loaf will rise to fifty pound.
What made Directors cheat in South-sea year?
To live on Ven'son when it sold so dear.[3]
Ask you why Phryne the whole Auction buys?
Phryne foresees a general Excise.
Why she and Sappho raise that monstrous sum?
Alas! they fear a man will cost a plum.[4]

    Wise Peter sees the World's respect for Gold,
And therefore hopes this Nation may be sold:[5]

1. Sir Gilbert Heathcote (1651–1733); Lord Mayor of London,
M.P., and Governor of the Bank of England.
2. See p. 154, n. 2.
3. In the extravagance and luxury of the South-Sea year, the price
of a haunch of venison was from three to five pounds. *P.* The
South-Sea Company collapsed in 1720, spreading financial ruin,
after fantastic sums had been realized.
4. £100,000.
5 Peter Walter (d. 1745); an attorney who acquired a vast fortune.

Glorious Ambition! Peter, swell thy store,
And be what Rome's great Didius[1] was before.

    The Crown of Poland, venal twice an age,
To just three millions stinted modest Gage.
But nobler scenes Maria's dreams unfold,[2]
Hereditary Realms, and worlds of Gold.
Congenial souls! whose life one Av'rice joins,
And one fate buries in th' Asturian Mines.

    Much-injur'd Blunt![3] why bears he Britain's hate?
A wizard told him in these words our fate:
'At length Corruption, like a gen'ral flood,
(So long by watchful Ministers withstood)
Shall deluge all; and Av'rice creeping on,
Spread like a low-born mist, and blot the Sun,
Statesman and Patriot ply alike the stocks,
Peeress and Butler share alike the Box,
And Judges job, and Bishops bite the town,
And mighty Dukes pack cards for half-a-crown.
See Britain sunk in lucre's sordid charms,
And France reveng'd of ANNE's and EDWARD's arms!'

1. A Roman lawyer, so rich as to purchase the Empire when it was set to sale upon the death of Pertinax. *P.*
2. The two persons mentioned were of quality, each of whom in the Missisippi [Scheme] despised to realise above three hundred thousand pounds; the gentleman with a view to the purchase of the crown of Poland, the lady on a vision of the like royal nature. They have since retired into Spain, where they are still in search of gold in the mines of the Asturias. *P.*
3. Sir John Blunt ... was one of the first projectors of the South-Sea Company, and afterwards one of the directors and chief managers of the famous scheme in 1720 ... Whether he did really credit the prophecy here mentioned is not certain, but it was constantly in this very style he declaimed against the corruption and luxury of the age ... He was patricularly eloquent against avarice in great and noble persons ... He died in the year 1732. *P.*

'Twas no Court-badge, great Scriv'ner! fir'd thy
    brain,
Nor lordly Luxury, nor City Gain:
No, 'twas thy righteous end, asham'd to see
Senates degen'rate, Patriots disagree,
And nobly wishing Party-rage to cease,
To buy both sides, and give thy Country peace.
   'All this is madness,' cries a sober sage:
But who, my friend, has reason in his rage?
'The Ruling Passion, be it what it will,
The Ruling Passion conquers Reason still.'
Less mad the wildest whimsy we can frame,
Than ev'n that Passion, if it has no Aim;
For though such motives Folly you may call,
The Folly's greater to have none at all.
   Hear, then, the truth: ''Tis Heav'n each Passion
    sends,
And diff'rent men directs to diff'rent ends.
Extremes in Nature equal good produce,
Extremes in Man concur to gen'ral use.'
Ask we what makes one keep, and one bestow?
That Pow'r who bids the Ocean ebb and flow,
Bids seed-time, harvest, equal course maintain,
Through reconcil'd extremes of drought and rain,
Builds Life on Death, on Change Duration founds,
And gives th' eternal wheels to know their rounds.
   Riches, like insects, when conceal'd they lie,
Wait but for wings, and in their season fly.
Who sees pale Mammon pine amidst his store,
Sees but a backward steward for the Poor;
This year a Reservoir, to keep and spare;
The next a Fountain, spouting through his Heir,
In lavish streams to quench a Country's thirst,
And men and dogs shall drink him till they burst.

Old Cotta sham'd his fortune and his birth,
Yet was not Cotta void of wit or worth:
What though (the use of barb'rous spits forgot)
His kitchen vy'd in coolness with his grot?
His court with nettles, moats with cresses stor'd,
With soups unbought and sallads bless'd his board?
If Cotta lived on pulse, it was no more
Than Bramins, Saints, and Sages did before;
To cram the Rich was prodigal expense,
And who would take the Poor from Providence?
Like some lone Chartreux stands the good old Hall,
Silence without, and Fasts within the wall;
No rafter'd roofs with dance and tabor sound,
No noontide-bell invites the country round:
Tenants with sighs the smokeless tow'rs survey,
And turn th' unwilling steeds another way:
Benighted wanderers, the forest o'er,
Curse the sav'd candle, and unop'ning door;
While the gaunt mastiff growling at the gate,
Affrights the beggar whom he longs to eat.

Not so his Son; he mark'd this oversight,
And then mistook reverse of wrong for right.
(For what to shun will no great knowledge need,
But what to follow, is a task indeed.)
Yet sure, of qualities deserving praise,
More go to ruin Fortunes, than to raise.
What slaughter'd hecatombs, what floods of wine,
Fill the capacious 'Squire, and deep Divine!
Yet no mean motive this profusion draws,
His oxen perish in his country's cause;
'Tis GEORGE and LIBERTY that crowns the cup,
And Zeal for that great House which eats him up.
The Woods recede around the naked seat,
The Sylvans groan – no matter – for the Fleet;

Next goes his Wool – to clothe our valiant bands,
Last, for his Country's Love, he sells his Lands.
To town he comes, completes the nation's hope,
And heads the bold Train-bands, and burns a Pope.
And shall not Britain now reward his toils,
Britain, that pays her Patriots with her Spoils?
In vain at Court the Bankrupt pleads his cause,
His thankless Country leaves him to her Laws.

    The Sense to value Riches, with the Art
T' enjoy them, and the Virtue to impart,
Not meanly, nor ambitiously pursu'd,
Not sunk by sloth, nor rais'd by servitude:
To balance Fortune by a just expense,
Join with Economy, Magnificence;
With Splendour, Charity; with Plenty, Health;
Oh teach us, BATHURST! yet unspoil'd by wealth!
That secret rare, between th' extremes to move
Of mad Good-nature and of mean Self-love.

    B. To Worth or Want well-weigh'd, be Bounty
      giv'n,
And ease, or emulate, the care of Heav'n;
(Whose measure full o'erflows on human race)
Mend Fortune's fault, and justify her grace.
Wealth in the gross is death, but life, diffus'd;
As Poison heals, in just proportion us'd:
In heaps, like Ambergrise, a stink it lies,
But well-dispers'd, is Incense to the Skies.

    P. Who starves by Nobles, or with Nobles eats?
The Wretch that trusts them, and the Rogue that
      cheats.
Is there a Lord, who knows a chearful noon
Without a Fiddler, Flatt'rer, or Buffoon?
Whose table, Wit, or modest Merit share,
Unelbow'd by a Gamester, Pimp, or Play'r?

Who copies Yours, or OXFORD's better part,[1]
To ease th' oppress'd, and raise the sinking heart?
Where'er he shines, Oh Fortune! gild the scene,
And Angels guard him in the golden Mean!
There, English Bounty yet a-while may stand,
And Honour linger e'er it leaves the land.

But all our praises why should Lords engross?
Rise, honest Muse! and sing the MAN of Ross:[2]
Pleas'd Vaga echoes through her winding bounds,
And rapid Severn hoarse applause resounds.
Who hung with woods yon mountain's sultry brow?
From the dry rock who bade the waters flow?
Not to the skies in useless columns tost,
Or in proud falls magnificently lost,
But clear and artless, pouring through the plain
Health to the sick, and solace to the swain.
Whose Causeway parts the vale with shady rows?
Whose Seats the weary Traveller repose?
Who taught that heav'n-directed spire to rise?
'The MAN of Ross' each lisping babe replies.
Behold the Market-place with poor o'erspread!
The MAN of Ross divides the weekly bread;
He feeds yon Alms-house, neat, but void of state,
Where Age and Want sit smiling at the gate:
Him portion'd maids, apprentic'd orphans blest,
The young who labour, and the old who rest.

1. See p. 89, n. 1.
2. The person here celebrated, who with a small estate actually performed all these good works, and whose true name was almost lost (partly by the title of the Man of Ross, given him by way of eminence, and partly by being buried without so much as an inscription), was called Mr John Kyrle. He died in the year 1724, aged 90, and lies interred in the chancel of the church of Ross, in Herefordshire. *P.* Kyrle executed his good works by raising subscriptions among his wealthy neighbours.

Is any sick? the MAN of Ross relieves,
Prescribes, attends, the med'cine makes, and gives.
Is there a variance? enter but his door,
Balk'd are the Courts, and contest is no more.
Despairing Quacks with curses fled the place,
And vile Attorneys, now a useless race.

    B. Thrice happy man! enabl'd to pursue
What all so wish, but want the pow'r to do!
Oh say, what sums that gen'rous hand supply?
What mines, to swell that boundless charity?

    P. Of Debts, and Taxes, Wife and Children clear
This man possest – five hundred pounds a year.
Blush, Grandeur, blush! proud Courts, withdraw your
    blaze!
Ye little Stars! hide your diminish'd rays.

    B. And what? no monument, inscription, stone?
His race, his form, his name almost unknown?

    P. Who builds a Church to God, and not to Fame,
Will never mark the marble with his Name:
Go, search it there, where to be born and die,
Of rich and poor makes all the history;[1]
Enough, that Virtue fill'd the space between;
Prov'd, by the ends of being, to have been.
When Hopkins dies, a thousand lights attend
The wretch, who living sav'd a candle's end:[2]
Should'ring God's altar a vile image stands,
Belies his features, nay extends his hands;
That live-long wig which Gorgon's self might own,
Eternal buckle takes in Parian stone.[3]

1. The Parish Register. *P.*
2. 'Vulture' Hopkins, see p. 152, n. 3.
3. The Poet ridicules the wretched taste of carving large periwigs on
   bustos, of which there are several vile examples in the tombs at
   Westminster and elsewhere. *P.*

Behold what blessings Wealth to life can lend!
And see, what comfort it affords our end.

In the worst inn's worst room, with mat half-hung,
The floors of plaister, and the walls of dung,
On once a flock-bed, but repair'd with straw,
With tape-ty'd curtains, never meant to draw,
The George and Garter dangling from that bed
Where tawdry yellow strove with dirty red,
Great Villiers[1] lies – alas! how chang'd from him,
That life of pleasure, and that soul of whim!
Gallant and gay, in Cliveden's proud alcove,[2]
The bow'r of wanton Shrewsbury and love;[3]
Or just as gay, at Council, in a ring
Of mimick, Statesmen, and their merry King.
No Wit to flatter, left of all his store!
No Fool to laugh at, which he valu'd more.
There, Victor of his health, of fortune, friends,
And fame; this lord of useless thousands ends.

His Grace's fate sage Cutler could foresee,[4]
And well (he thought) advis'd him, 'Live like me.'
As well his Grace reply'd, 'Like you, Sir John?
That I can do, when all I have is gone.'

---

1. This lord [George Villiers, Duke of Buckingham], yet more famous for his vices than his misfortunes, having been possessed of about £50,000 a year, and passing through many of the highest posts in the kingdom, died in the year 1687, in a remote inn in Yorkshire, reduced to the utmost misery. *P.*

2. A delightful palace on the banks of the Thames, built by the Duke of Buckingham. *P.*

3. The Countess of Shrewsbury, a woman abandoned to gallantries. The Earl, her husband, was killed by the Duke of Buckingham in a duel; and it has been said, that during the combat she held the Duke's horses, in the habit of a page. *P.*

4. Sir John Cutler (1608?–93); personally parsimonious, yet a public benefactor.

Resolve me, Reason, which of these is worse,
Want with a full, or with an empty purse?
Thy life more wretched, Cutler, was confess'd,
Arise, and tell me, was thy death more bless'd?
Cutler saw tenants break, and houses fall;
For very want; he could not build a wall.
His only daughter in a stranger's pow'r,
For very want; he could not pay a dow'r.
A few grey hairs his rev'rend temples crown'd,
'Twas very want that sold them for two pound.
What ev'n deny'd a cordial at his end,
Banish'd the doctor, and expell'd the friend?
What but a want, which you perhaps think mad,
Yet numbers feel, the want of what he had!
Cutler and Brutus, dying both exclaim,
'Virtue! and Wealth! what are ye but a name!'
  Say, for such worth are other worlds prepar'd?
Or are they both, in this their own reward?
A knotty point! to which we now proceed.
But you are tir'd – I'll tell a tale –
  B.   Agreed.
  P. Where London's column,[1] pointing at the skies
Like a tall bully, lifts the head, and lies;
There dwelt a Citizen of sober fame,
A plain good man, and Balaam was his name;
Religious, punctual, frugal, and so forth;
His word would pass for more than he was worth.
One solid dish his week-day meal affords,
An added pudding solemnis'd the Lord's:
Constant at Church, and 'Change; his gains were
      sure,
His givings rare, save farthings to the poor.

---

1. The Monument, built in memory of the fire of London, with an
   inscription importing that city to have been burnt by the Papists. *P*.

The Dev'l was piqu'd such saintship to behold,
And long'd to tempt him like good Job of old:
But Satan now is wiser than of yore,
And tempts by making rich, not making poor.

Rouz'd by the Prince of Air, the whirlwinds sweep
The surge, and plunge his Father in the deep;
Then full against his Cornish lands they roar,
And two rich shipwrecks bless the lucky shore.

Sir Balaam now, he lives like other folks,
He takes his chirping pint, and cracks his jokes:
'Live like yourself,' was soon my Lady's word;
And, lo! two puddings smok'd upon the board.

Asleep and naked as an Indian lay,
An honest factor stole a Gem away:
He pledg'd it to the Knight, the Knight had wit,
So kept the Di'mond, and the rogue was bit.
Some scruple rose, but thus he eas'd his thought,
'I'll now give six-pence where I gave a groat;
Where once I went to church, I'll now go twice –
And am so clear too of all other vice.'

The Tempter saw his time; the work he ply'd;
Stocks and Subscriptions pour on ev'ry side,
Till all the Demon makes his full descent
In one abundant show'r of Cent per Cent,
Sinks deep within him, and possesses whole,
Then dubs Director, and secures his soul.

Behold Sir Balaam, now a man of spirit,
Ascribes his gettings to his parts and merit;
What late he call'd a Blessing, now was Wit,
And God's good Providence, a lucky Hit.
Things change their titles, as our manners turn:
His Compting-house employ'd the Sunday-morn;
Seldom at church ('twas such a busy life)
But duly sent his family and wife.

There (so the Dev'l ordain'd) one Christmas-tide,
My good old Lady catch'd a cold, and dy'd.

   A Nymph of Quality admires our Knight;
He marries, bows at Court, and grows polite:
Leaves the dull Cits, and joins (to please the fair)
The well-bred cuckolds in St James's air:
First, for his Son a gay Commission buys,
Who drinks, whores, fights, and in a duel dies:
His Daughter flaunts a Viscount's tawdry wife;
She bears a Coronet and P – x for life.
In Britain's Senate he a seat obtains,
And one more Pensioner St Stephen gains.
My Lady falls to play; so bad her chance,
He must repair it; takes a bribe from France;
The House impeach him; Coningsby harangues;[1]
The Court forsake him – and Sir Balaam hangs:
Wife, son, and daughter, Satan! are thy own,
His wealth, yet dearer, forfeit to the Crown:
The Devil and the King divide the Prize,
And sad Sir Balaam curses God, and dies.

EPISTLE IV

TO RICHARD BOYLE, EARL OF BURLINGTON[2]

Of the Use of RICHES

'TIS strange, the Miser should his Cares employ
To gain those Riches he can ne'er enjoy:

---

1. Thomas, Earl of Coningsby (1656?–1729); an M.P. and notable politician.
2. Richard Boyle, third Earl of Burlington (1695–1753); statesman; patron of literature and art.

Is it less strange, the Prodigal should waste
His wealth, to purchase what he ne'er can taste?
Not for himself he sees, or hears, or eats;
Artists must choose his Pictures, Music, Meats;
He buys for Topham, Drawings and Designs,[1]
For Pembroke, Statues, dirty Gods, and Coins;[2]
Rare monkish Manuscripts for Hearne alone,[3]
And Books for Mead, and Butterflies for Sloane.[4]
Think we all these are for himself? no more
Than his fine Wife, alas! or finer Whore.

For what has Virro painted, built, and planted?
Only to show, how many Tastes he wanted.
What brought Sir Visto's ill-got wealth to waste?
Some Demon whisper'd, 'Visto! have a taste.'
Heav'n visits with a Taste the wealthy fool,
And needs no Rod but Ripley with a Rule.[5]
See! sportive fate, to punish awkward pride,
Bids Bubo build, and sends him such a Guide:
A standing sermon, at each year's expense,
That never Coxcomb reach'd Magnificence!

You show us, Rome was glorious, not profuse,[6]
And pompous buildings once were things of Use.

1. A gentleman famous for a judicious collection of drawings. *P.*
2. Thomas Herbert, eighth Earl of Pembroke (1656–1733); states-
man.
3. Thomas Hearne (1678–1735); antiquary.
4. Two eminent physicians; the one had an excellent library, the other
the finest collection in Europe of natural curiosities; both men of
great learning and humanity. *P.*
5. This man was a carpenter, employed by a first Minister, who
raised him to be an Architect, without any genius in the art; and
after some wretched proofs of his insufficiency in public buildings
made him Comptroller of the Board of Works. *P.*
6. The Earl of Burlington was then publishing the Designs of Inigo
Jones, and the Antiquities of Rome by Palladio. *P.*

Yet shall (my Lord) your just, your noble rules,
Fill half the land with Imitating-Fools;
Who random drawings from your sheets shall take,
And of one beauty many blunders make;
Load some vain Church with old Theatric state,
Turn Arcs of triumph to a Garden-gate;
Reverse your Ornaments; and hang them all
On some patch'd dog-hole ek'd with ends of wall;
Then clap four slices of Pilaster on 't,
That, lac'd with bits of rustic, makes a Front.
Shall call the winds through long arcades to roar,
Proud to catch cold at a Venetian door;
Conscious they act a true Palladian part,
And if they starve, they starve by rules of art.

Oft have you hinted to your brother Peer,
A certain truth, which many buy too dear:
Something there is more needful than Expense,
And something previous ev'n to Taste – 'tis Sense:
Good Sense, which only is the gift of Heav'n,
And though no Science, fairly worth the seven:
A Light, which in yourself you must perceive;
Jones and Le Nôtre have it not to give.[1]

To build, to plant, whatever you intend,
To rear the Column, or the Arch to bend,
To swell the Terrace, or to sink the Grot;
In all, let Nature never be forgot.
But treat the Goddess like a modest fair,
Nor over-dress, nor leave her wholly bare;
Let not each beauty ev'ry where be spy'd,
Where half the skill is decently to hide.
He gains all points, who pleasingly confounds,
Surprises, varies, and conceals the Bounds.

1. Inigo Jones, the celebrated architect; and M. le Nôtre, the de-
signer of the best gardens in France. *P.*

Consult the Genius of the Place in all;
That tells the Waters or to rise, or fall;
Or helps th' ambitious Hill the heav'ns to scale,
Or scoops in circling theatres the Vale;
Calls in the Country, catches op'ning Glades,
Joins willing Woods, and varies Shades from Shades;
Now breaks, or now directs, th' intending Lines;
Paints as you plant, and, as you work, designs.

Still follow Sense, of ev'ry art the soul,
Parts answ'ring parts shall slide into a whole,
Spontaneous beauties all around advance,
Start ev'n from Difficulty, strike from Chance;
Nature shall join you; Time shall make it grow
A Work to wonder at – perhaps a STOWE.[1]

Without it, proud Versailles! thy glory falls;
And Nero's Terraces desert their walls:
The vast Parterres a thousand hands shall make,
Lo! COBHAM comes, and floats them with a Lake:
Or cut wide views through Mountains to the Plain,
You'll wish your hill or shelter'd seat again.
Ev'n in an ornament its place remark,
Nor in an Hermitage set Dr Clarke.[2]

Behold Villario's ten-years toil complete;
His Quincunx darkens, his Espaliers meet;
The Wood supports the Plain, the parts unite,
And strength of Shade contends with strength of
    Light;
A waving Glow the blooming beds display,
Blushing in bright diversities of day,

1. The seat and gardens of Lord Viscount Cobham, in Buckingham-
shire. *P.*
2. Dr S. Clarke's bust was placed by the Queen in the Hermitage,
while the doctor duly frequented the Court. *P.* Samuel Clarke
(1675–1729); theologian.

With silver-quiv'ring rills meander'd o'er –
Enjoy them, you! Villario can no more;
Tired of the scene Parterres and Fountains yield,
He finds at last, he better likes a Field.
   Through his young Woods how pleased Sabinus
      stray'd,
Or sat delighted in the thick'ning shade,
With annual joy the red'ning shoots to greet,
Or see the stretching branches long to meet!
His Son's fine Taste an op'ner Vista loves,
Foe to the Dryads of his Father's groves;
One boundless Green, or flourish'd Carpet views,
With all the mournful family of Yews;
The thriving plants, ignoble broomsticks made,
Now sweep those Alleys they were born to shade.
   At Timon's Villa[1] let us pass a day,
Where all cry out, 'What sums are thrown away!'
So proud, so grand; of that stupendous air,
Soft and Agreeable come never there.
Greatness, with Timon, dwells in such a draught
As brings all Brobdignag before your thought.
To compass this, his building is a Town,
His pond an Ocean, his parterre a Down:
Who but must laugh, the Master when he sees,
A puny insect, shiv'ring at a breeze!
Lo, what huge heaps of littleness around!
The whole, a labour'd Quarry above ground.
Two Cupids squirt before: a Lake behind
Improves the keenness of the Northern wind.
His Gardens next your admiration call,
On ev'ry side you look, behold the Wall!

---

1. This was accepted as a description of the Duke of Chandos's seat
at Canons. See p. 131, n. 1.

No pleasing Intricacies intervene,
No artful wildness to perplex the scene;
Grove nods at grove, each Alley has a brother,
And half the platform just reflects the other.
The suff'ring eye inverted Nature sees,
Trees cut to Statues, Statues thick as trees;
With here a Fountain, never to be play'd;
And there a Summer-house, that knows no shade;
Here Amphitrite sails through myrtle bow'rs;
There Gladiators fight, or die in flow'rs;
Unwater'd see the drooping sea-horse mourn,
And swallows roost in Nilus' dusty Urn.

My Lord advances with majestic mien,
Smit with the mighty pleasure, to be seen:
But soft – by regular approach – not yet –
First thro' the length of yon hot Terrace sweat;
And when up ten steep slopes you've drag'd your
    thighs,
Just at his Study-door he'll bless your eyes.

His Study! with what Authors is it stor'd?[1]
In Books, not Authors, curious is my Lord;
To all their dated backs he turns you round;
These Aldus printed, those Du Suëil has bound!
Lo some are Vellum, and the rest as good
For all his Lordship knows, but they are Wood.
For Locke or Milton 'tis in vain to look,
These shelves admit not any modern Book.

And now the Chapel's silver bell you hear,
That summons you to all the Pride of Pray'r:

1. The false taste in books; a satire on the vanity of collecting them,
more frequent in men of fortune than the study to understand
them. Many delight chiefly in the elegance of the print or binding;
some have carried it so far as to cause the upper shelves to be filled
with painted books of wood ... *P.*

Light quirks of Music, broken and uneven,
Make the soul dance upon a Jig to Heav'n.
On painted cielings you devoutly stare,
Where sprawl the Saints of Verrio or Laguerre,[1]
On gilded clouds in fair expansion lie,
And bring all Paradise before your eye.
To rest, the Cushion and soft Dean invite,
Who never mentions Hell to ears polite.

But hark! the chiming Clocks to dinner call;
A hundred footsteps scrape the marble Hall:
The rich Buffet well-colour'd Serpents grace,
And gaping Tritons spew to wash your face.
Is this a dinner? this a Genial room?
No, 'tis a Temple, and a Hecatomb.
A solemn Sacrifice, perform'd in state,
You drink by measure, and to minutes eat.
So quick retires each flying course, you'd swear
Sancho's dread Doctor and his Wand were there.
Between each Act the trembling salvers ring,
From soup to sweet-wine, and God bless the King.
In plenty starving, tantaliz'd in state,
And complaisantly help'd to all I hate,
Treated, caress'd, and tir'd, I take my leave,
Sick of his civil Pride from Morn to Eve;
I curse such lavish cost, and little skill,
And swear no Day was ever past so ill.

Yet hence the Poor are cloath'd, the Hungry fed;
Health to himself, and to his Infants bread
The Lab'rer bears: What his hard Heart denies,
His charitable Vanity supplies.

---

1. Verrio (Antonio) painted many cielings, etc., at Windsor, Hampton Court, etc., and Laguerre at Blenheim Castle and other places. *P.*

Another Age shall see the golden Ear
Imbrown the Slope, and nod on the Parterre,
Deep Harvests bury all his pride has plann'd,
And laughing Ceres re-assume the land.

Who then shall grace, or who improve the Soil?
Who plants like BATHURST, or who builds like BOYLE.
'Tis Use alone that sanctifies Expense,
And Splendour borrows all her rays from Sense.

His Father's Acres who enjoys in peace,
Or makes his Neighbours glad, if he increase:
Whose chearful Tenants bless their yearly toil,
Yet to their Lord owe more than to the soil;
Whose ample Lawns are not asham'd to feed
The milky heifer, and deserving steed;
Whose rising Forests, not for pride or show,
But future Buildings, future Navies, grow:
Let his plantations stretch from down to down,
First shade a Country, and then raise a Town.

You too proceed! make falling Arts your care,
Erect new wonders, and the old repair;
Jones and Palladio to themselves restore,
And be whate'er Vitruvius was before:[1]
Till Kings call forth th' Ideas of your mind,
(Proud to accomplish what such hands design'd)
Bid Harbours open, public Ways extend,
Bid Temples, worthier of the God, ascend;
Bid the broad Arch the dang'rous Flood contain,
The Mole projected break the roaring Main;
Back to his bounds their subject Sea command,
And roll obedient Rivers through the Land;
These Honours, Peace to happy Britain brings,
These are Imperial Works, and worthy Kings.

---

1. M. Vitruvius Pollio (80 B.C.) who wrote on architecture.

EPISTLE TO DR ARBUTHNOT

BEING THE PROLOGUE TO THE SATIRES

P. SHUT, shut the door, good John![1] fatigu'd I
    said,
Tye up the knocker, say I'm sick, I'm dead.
The Dog-star rages! nay, 'tis past a doubt,
All Bedlam, or Parnassus, is let out:
Fire in each eye, and papers in each hand,
They rave, recite, and madden round the land.

    What walls can guard me, or what shades can hide?
They pierce my Thickets, through my Grot they glide,
By land, by water, they renew the charge,
They stop the chariot, and they board the barge.
No place is sacred, not the Church is free,
Ev'n Sunday shines no Sabbath-day to me:
Then from the Mint[2] walks forth the Man of rhyme,
Happy! to catch me, just at Dinner-time.

    Is there a Parson, much be-mus'd in beer,
A maudlin Poetess, a rhyming Peer,
A Clerk, foredoom'd his father's soul to cross,
Who pens a Stanza, when he should *engross*?
Is there, who, lock'd from ink and paper, scrawls
With desp'rate charcoal round his darken'd walls?
All fly to TWIT'NAM, and in humble strain
Apply to me, to keep them mad or vain.
Arthur, whose giddy son neglects the laws,
Imputes to me and my damn'd works the cause:
Poor Cornus sees his frantic wife elope,
And curses Wit, and Poetry, and Pope.

1. John Searle, Pope's servant.
2. A sanctuary for insolvent debtors in Southwark.

Friend to my life! (which did not you prolong,
The world had wanted many an idle song)
What *Drop* or *Nostrum* can this plague remove?
Or which must end me, a Fool's wrath or love?
A dire dilemma! either way I'm sped,
If foes, they write, if friends, they read me dead.
Seiz'd and ty'd down to judge, how wretched I?
Who can't be silent, and who will not lie:
To laugh, were want of goodness and of grace,
And to be grave, exceeds all Pow'r of face.
I sit with sad civility, I read
With honest anguish, and an aching head;
And drop at last, but in unwilling ears,
This saving counsel, 'Keep your piece nine years.'

'Nine years!' cries he, who high in Drury-lane,
Lull'd by soft Zephyrs through the broken pane,
Rhymes ere he wakes, and prints before *Term* ends,
Oblig'd by hunger, and request of friends:
'The piece, you think, is incorrect? why take it,
I'm all submission, what you'd have it, make it.'

Three things another's modest wishes bound,
My Friendship, and a Prologue, and ten pound.
Pitholeon[1] sends to me: 'You know his Grace,
I want a Patron; ask him for a Place.'
Pitholeon libell'd me – 'But here's a letter
Informs you, Sir, 'twas when he knew no better.
Dare you refuse him? Curl invites to dine,[2]
He'll write a *Journal*, or he'll turn Divine.'

Bless me! a packet. – ''Tis a stranger sues,
A Virgin Tragedy, an Orphan Muse.'

1. The name taken from a foolish poet of Rhodes, who pretended
much to Greek. *P.*
2. Edmund Curll (1675–1747), a notorious bookseller and an
enemy of Pope's.

If I dislike it, 'Furies, death and rage!'
If I approve, 'Commend it to the Stage.'
There (thank my stars) my whole commission ends,
The Play'rs and I are, luckily, no friends.
Fir'd that the house reject him, ''Sdeath! I'll print it,
And shame the fools — Your int'rest, Sir, with
    Lintot.'[1]
Lintot, dull rogue! will think your price too much:
'Not, Sir, if you revise it, and retouch.'
All my demurs but double his attacks;
At last he whispers, 'Do; and we go snacks.'
Glad of a quarrel, straight I clap the door,
Sir, let me see your works and you no more.

   'Tis sung, when Midas' Ears began to spring
(Midas, a sacred person and a King),
His very Minister who spy'd them first,
(Some say his Queen) was forc'd to speak, or burst.
And is not mine, my friend, a sorer case,
When ev'ry coxcomb perks them in my face?
   A. Good friend, forbear! you deal in dang'rous
    things.
I'd never name Queens, Ministers, or Kings;
Keep close to Ears, and those let asses prick,
'Tis nothing——
   P.   Nothing? if they bite and kick?
Out with it, Dunciad! let the secret pass,
That secret to each fool, that he's an Ass:
The truth once told (and wherefore should we lie?)
The Queen of Midas slept, and so may I.

   You think this cruel? take it for a rule,
No creature smarts so little as a fool.
Let peals of laughter, Codrus! round thee break,
Thou unconcern'd canst hear the mighty crack:

1. A contemporary bookseller.

Pit, box, and gall'ry in convulsions hurl'd,
Thou stand'st unshook amidst a bursting world.
Who shames a Scribbler? break one cobweb thro',
He spins the slight, self-pleasing thread anew:
Destroy his fib, or sophistry, in vain,
The creature's at his dirty work again,
Thron'd in the centre of his thin designs,
Proud of a vast extent of flimsy lines!
Whom have I hurt? has Poet yet, or Peer,
Lost the arch'd eye-brow, or Parnassian sneer?
And has not Colley still his lord, and whore?[1]
His butchers, Henley,[2] his free-masons, Moore?[3]
Does not one table Bavius still admit?
Still to one Bishop, Philips seem a wit?[4]
Still Sappho——

   A.   Hold! for God-sake – you'll offend,
No Names – be calm – learn prudence of a friend:
I too could write, and I am twice as tall;
But foes like these——

   P.   One Flatt'rer's worse than all.
Of all mad creatures, if the learn'd are right,
It is the slaver kills, and not the bite.
A fool quite angry is quite innocent:
Alas! 'tis ten times worse when they *repent*.

  One dedicates in high heroic prose,
And ridicules beyond a hundred foes:
One from all Grubstreet will my fame defend,
And more abusive, calls himself my friend.
This prints my *Letters*, that expects a bribe,
And others roar aloud, 'Subscribe, subscribe.'

1. Colley Cibber (1671–1757); actor, dramatist, and poet laureate.
2. John Henley (1692–1756); popular preacher and orator.
3. James Moore Smyth (1702–34); a poor poet and enemy of Pope.
4. Ambrose Philips (1675–1749); a fine poet, was secretary to the Bishop of Armagh.

There are, who to my person pay their court:
I cough like *Horace*, and, tho' lean, am short,
Ammon's[1] great son one shoulder had too high,
Such *Ovid's* nose, and, 'Sir! you have an Eye' –
Go on, obliging creatures, make me see,
All that disgrac'd my Betters, met in me.
Say for my comfort, languishing in bed,
'Just so immortal *Maro* held his head:'
And when I die, be sure you let me know
Great *Homer* died three thousand years ago.

Why did I write? what sin to me unknown
Dipt me in ink, my parents', or my own?
As yet a child, nor yet a fool to fame,
I lisp'd in numbers, for the numbers came.
I left no calling for this idle trade,
No duty broke, no father disobey'd.
The Muse but serv'd to ease some friend, not
   Wife,
To help me through this long disease, my Life,
To second, ARBUTHNOT! thy Art and Care,
And teach the Being you preserv'd, to bear.

But why then publish? *Granville*[2] the polite
And knowing *Walsh*,[3] would tell me I could write;
Well-natur'd *Garth* inflam'd with early praise,
And *Congreve* lov'd, and *Swift* endur'd my lays;
The courtly *Talbot, Somers, Sheffield* read,
Ev'n mitred *Rochester* would nod the head,
And *St John's* self (great *Dryden's* friends
   before)[4]
With open arms receiv'd one Poet more.
Happy my studies, when by these approv'd!
Happier their author, when by these belov'd!

1. Alexander the Great.   2. See p. 2, n. 3.   3. See p. 10, n. 1.
4. All these were patrons or admirers of Mr Dryden ... *P.*

From these the world will judge of men and books,
Not from the *Burnets*, *Oldmixons*, and *Cooks*.[1]

    Soft were my numbers; who could take offence
While pure Description held the place of Sense?
Like gentle *Fanny's* was my flow'ry theme,
A painted mistress, or a purling stream.
Yet then did *Gildon*[2] draw his venal quill;
I wish'd the man a Dinner, and sat still..
Yet then did *Dennis* rave in furious fret;[3]
I never answer'd – I was not in debt.
If want provok'd, or madness made them print,
I wag'd no war with *Bedlam* or the *Mint*.

    Did some more sober Critic come abroad;
If wrong, I smil'd; if right, I kiss'd the rod.
Pains, reading, study, are their just pretence,
And all they want is spirit, taste, and sense.
Commas and points they set exactly right,
And 'twere a sin to rob them of their mite.
Yet ne'er one sprig of laurel grac'd these ribalds,
From slashing *Bentley* down to piddling *Tibbalds*:[4]
Each wight who reads not, and but scans and spells,
Each Word-catcher, that lives on syllables,
Ev'n such small Critics some regard may claim,
Preserved in *Milton's* or in *Shakespeare's* name.
Pretty! in amber to observe the forms
Of hairs, or straws, or dirt, or grubs, or worms!
The things, we know, are neither rich nor rare,
But wonder how the devil they got there.

1. Authors of secret and scandalous history. *P*.
2. Charles Gildon (1665–1724); author, and detractor of Pope.
3. John Dennis (1657–1734); critic and dramatist.
4. Richard Bentley (1662–1742); the great scholar, published a bad edition of Milton. Lewis Theobald (1688–1744); scholar, edited Shakespeare and criticised Pope's edition that appeared in 1725.

Were others angry: I excus'd them too;
Well might they rage, I gave them but their due.
A man's true merit 'tis not hard to find;
But each man's secret standard in his mind,
That Casting-weight pride adds to emptiness,
This, who can gratify? for who can *guess*?
The Bard whom pilfer'd Pastorals renown,
Who turns a Persian tale for half a Crown,
Just writes to make his barrenness appear,
And strains, from hard-bound brains, eight lines a
        year;
He, who still wanting, tho' he lives on theft,
Steals much, spends little, yet has nothing left:
And He, who now to sense, now nonsense leaning,
Means not, but blunders round about a meaning:
And He, whose fustian's so sublimely bad,
It is not Poetry, but prose run mad:
All these, my modest Satire bade *translate*,
And own'd that nine such Poets made a *Tate*.[1]
How did they fume, and stamp, and roar, and chafe!
And swear, not ADDISON[2] himself was safe

    Peace to all such! but were there One whose fires
True Genius kindles, and fair Fame inspires;
Blest with each talent and each art to please,
And born to write, converse, and live with ease:
Should such a man, too fond to rule alone,
Bear, like the Turk, no brother near the throne,
View him with scornful, yet with jealous eyes,
And hate for arts that caus'd himself to rise;
Damn with faint praise, assent with civil leer,
And, without sneering, teach the rest to sneer;
Willing to wound, and yet afraid to strike,
Just hint a fault, and hesitate dislike;

1. Nahum Tate (1652–1715); a dull poet.   2. See p. 99, n. 1.

Alike reserv'd to blame, or to commend,
A tim'rous foe, and a suspicious friend;
Dreading ev'n fools, by Flatterers besieged,
And so obliging, that he ne'er oblig'd;
Like *Cato*, give his little Senate laws,
And sit attentive to his own applause;
While Wits and Templars ev'ry sentence raise,
And wonder with a foolish face of praise –
Who but must laugh, if such a man there be?
Who would not weep, if ATTICUS were he?

What tho' my Name stood rubric on the walls,
Or plaister'd posts, with claps, in capitals?[1]
Or smoking forth, a hundred hawkers load,
On wings of winds came flying all abroad?
I sought no homage from the Race that write;
I kept, like *Asian* Monarchs, from their sight:
Poems I heeded (now be-rhym'd so long)
No more than thou, great GEORGE! a birthday song.[2]
I ne'er with wits or witlings pass'd my days,
To spread about the itch of verse and praise;
Nor like a puppy, daggled through the town,
To fetch and carry sing-song up and down;
Nor at Rehearsals sweat, and mouth'd, and cry'd,
With handkerchief and orange at my side;
But sick of fops, and poetry, and prate,
To *Bufo* left the whole Castalian state.

Proud as *Apollo* on his forked hill,
Sat full-blown *Bufo*, puff'd by ev'ry quill;
Fed with soft Dedication all day long,
Horace and he went hand in hand in song.
His Library (where busts of Poets dead
And a true *Pindar* stood without a head)

1. Booksellers advertised their books by hanging up the title-pages.
2. The laureate addressed a poem to the king on his birthday.

Receiv'd of wits an undistinguish'd race,
Who first his judgment ask'd, and then a place:
Much they extoll'd his pictures, much his seat,
And flatter'd ev'ry day, and some days eat:
Till grown more frugal in his riper days,
He paid some bards with port, and some with praise,
To some a dry rehearsal was assign'd,
And others (harder still) he paid in kind.
Dryden alone (what wonder?) came not nigh,
Dryden alone escap'd this judging eye:
But still the *Great* have kindness in reserve,
He help'd to bury whom he help'd to starve.
    May some choice patron bless each gray-goose
      quill!
May every *Bavius* have his *Bufo* still!
So when a Statesman wants a day's defence,
Or Envy holds a whole week's war with Sense,
Or simple pride for flatt'ry makes demands,
May dunce by dunce be whistled off my hands!
Bless'd be the *Great*! for those they take away,
And those they left me; for they left me GAY;[1]
Left me to see neglected Genius bloom,
Neglected die, and tell it on his tomb:
Of all thy blameless life, the sole return
My Verse, and QUEENSB'RY[2] weeping o'er thy urn!
    Oh let me live my own, and die so too!
(To live and die is all I have to do:)
Maintain a Poet's dignity and ease,
And see what friends, and read what books I please:
Above a Patron, tho' I condescend
Sometimes to call a Minister my friend.
I was not born for Courts or great affairs;
I pay my debts, believe, and say my pray'rs;

1. See p. 85, n. 1.   2. See p. 145, n. 1.

Can sleep without a Poem in my head,
Nor know if *Dennis*[1] be alive or dead.

Why am I ask'd what next shall see the light?
Heav'ns! was I born for nothing but to write?
Has Life no joys for me? or (to be grave)
Have I no friend to serve, no soul to save?
'I found him close with *Swift*[2] – Indeed? no doubt
(Cries prating *Balbus*) something will come out.'
'Tis all in vain, deny it as I will.
'No, such a Genius never can lie still;'
And then for mine obligingly mistakes
The first lampoon Sir *Will*. or *Bubo* makes.
Poor guiltless I! and can I choose but smile,
When ev'ry Coxcomb knows me by my *Style*?

Curst be the verse, how well soe'er it flow,
That tends to make one worthy man my foe,
Give Virtue scandal, Innocence a fear,
Or from the soft-ey'd Virgin steal a tear!
But he who hurts a harmless neighbour's peace,
Insults fall'n worth, or Beauty in distress,
Who loves a Lie, lame Slander helps about,
Who writes a Libel, or who copies out:
That Fop, whose pride affects a patron's name,
Yet, absent, wounds an author's honest fame:
Who can *your* merit *selfishly* approve,
And show the *sense* of it without the *love*;
Who has the vanity to call you friend,
Yet wants the honour, injur'd, to defend;
Who tells whate'er you think, whate'er you say,
And, if he lie not, must at least betray:

1. See p. 176, n. 3.   2. See p. 89, n. 2

Who to the *Dean*, and *silver bell* can swear,[1]
And sees at *Cannons* what was never there;
Who reads, but with a lust to misapply,
Make Satire a Lampoon, and Fiction Lie;
A lash like mine no honest man shall dread,
But all such babling blockheads in his stead.
Let *Sporus*[2] tremble——

    A.   What? that thing of silk,
Sporus, that mere white curd of Ass's milk?
Satire or Sense, alas! can *Sporus* feel?
Who breaks a butterfly upon a wheel?

    P. Yet let me flap this bug with gilded wings,
This painted child of dirt, that stinks and stings;
Whose buzz the witty and the fair annoys,
Yet wit ne'er tastes, and beauty ne'er enjoys:
So well-bred spaniels civilly delight
In mumbling of the game they dare not bite.
Eternal smiles his emptiness betray,
As shallow streams run dimpling all the way.
Whether in florid impotence he speaks,
And, as the prompter breathes, the puppet squeaks;
Or at the ear of *Eve*, familiar Toad!
Half froth, half venom, spits himself abroad,
In puns or politics, or tales, or lies,
Or spite, or smut, or rhymes, or blasphemies.
His wit all see-saw, between *that* and *this*,
Now high, now low, now master up, now miss,
And he himself one vile Antithesis.

---

1. Meaning the man who would have the Duke of Chandos that Mr Pope meant him in those circumstances ridiculed in the Epistle on Taste ... *P. Timon's Villa* was interpreted to be the Duke of Chandos's seat at *Cannons*. See p. 167, n. 1.
2. Sporus is John Lord Hervey (1696–1743); courtier, author, and scurrilous defamer of Pope.

Amphibious thing! that, acting either part,
The trifling head, or the corrupted heart,
Fop at the toilet, flatt'rer at the board,
Now trips a Lady, and now struts a Lord.
Eve's tempter thus the Rabbins have express'd,
A Cherub's face, a reptile all the rest,
Beauty that shocks you, parts that none will trust,
Wit that can creep, and pride that licks the dust.

  Not Fortune's worshipper, nor Fashion's fool,
Not Lucre's madman, nor Ambition's tool,
Not proud, nor servile; be one Poet's praise,
That, if he pleas'd, he pleas'd by manly ways:
That Flatt'ry, even to Kings, he held a shame,
And thought a Lie in verse or prose the same.
That not in Fancy's maze he wander'd long,
But stoop'd to Truth, and moraliz'd his song:
That not for Fame, but Virtue's better end,
He stood the furious foe, the timid friend,
The damning critic, half-approving wit,
The coxcomb hit, or fearing to be hit;
Laugh'd at the loss of friends he never had,
The dull, the proud, the wicked, and the mad;
The distant threats of vengeance on his head,
The blow unfelt, the tear he never shed;
The tale revived, the lie so oft o'erthrown,
Th' imputed trash, and dulness not his own;
The morals blacken'd when the writings 'scape,
The libell'd person, and the pictur'd shape;
Abuse, on all he lov'd, or lov'd him, spread,
A friend in exile, or a father, dead;
The whisper, that to greatness still too near,
Perhaps yet vibrates on his Sov'REIGN's ear —
Welcome for thee, fair Virtue! all the past:
For thee, fair Virtue! welcome ev'n the *last*!

A. But why insult the poor, affront the great?
P. A knave's a knave, to me, in ev'ry state:
Alike my scorn, if he succeed or fail,
Sporus at court, or *Japhet*[1] in a jail,
A hireling scribbler, or a hireling peer,
Knight of the post corrupt, or of the shire;
If on a Pillory, or near a Throne,
He gain his Prince's ear, or lose his own,
    Yet soft by nature, more a dupe than wit,
Sappho can tell you how this man was bit:
This dreaded Sat'rist *Dennis*[2] will confess
Foe to his pride, but Friend to his distress:
So humble, he has knock'd at *Tibbald's*[3] door,
Has drunk with *Cibber*,[4] nay, has rhymed for *Moor*.[5]
Full ten years slander'd, did he once reply?
Three thousand suns went down on *Welsted's* lie.[6]
To please his Mistress one aspers'd his life;
He lash'd him not, but let her be his wife:
Let *Budgel* charge low *Grubstreet* on his quill,[7]
And write whate'er he pleas'd, except his Will;
Let the two *Curls*[8] of Town and Court abuse
His father, mother, body, soul, and muse.
Yet why? that Father held it for a rule,
It was a sin to call our neighbour fool:
That harmless Mother thought no wife a whore;
Hear this, and spare his family, *James Moore*![9]
Unspotted names, and memorable long!
If there be force in Virtue, or in Song.

1. See p. 152, n. 4.   2. See p. 176, n. 3.   3. See p. 176, n. 4.
4. See p. 174, n. 1.   5. See p. 174, n. 3.
6. This man had the impudence to tell in print that Mr P. had oc-
   casioned a *Lady's death* ... *P.*
7. Budgel, in a weekly pamphlet called the Bee, bestowed much
   abuse on him ... *P.*
8. Edmund Curll, the bookseller, see p. 99, n. 2; and Lord Hervey,
   the courtier, see p. 181, n. 2.   9. See p. 174, n. 3.

Of gentle blood (part shed in Honour's cause,
While yet in *Britain* Honour had applause)
Each parent sprung——

A.   What fortune, pray?——

P.   Their own,

And better got, than *Bestia's* from the throne.
Born to no Pride, inheriting no Strife,
Nor marrying Discord in a noble wife,
Stranger to civil and religious rage,
The good man walk'd innoxious through his age.
No Courts he saw, no suits would ever try,
Nor dar'd an Oath, nor hazarded a Lie.
Unlearn'd, he knew no schoolman's subtle art,
No language but the language of the heart.
By Nature honest, by Experience wise,
Healthy by temp'rance, and by exercise;
His life, tho' long, to sickness past unknown,
His death was instant, and without a groan,
O grant me, thus to live, and thus to die!
Who sprung from Kings shall know less joy than I.

O Friend! may each domestic bliss be thine!
Be no unpleasing Melancholy mine:
Me, let the tender office long engage,
To rock the cradle of reposing Age,
With lenient arts extend a Mother's breath,
Make Languor smile, and smooth the bed of Death,
Explore the thought, explain the asking eye,
And keep a while one parent from the sky!
On cares like these, if length of days attend,
May Heav'n, to bless those days, preserve my friend,
Preserve him social, cheerful, and serene,
And just as rich as when he serv'd a QUEEN.[1]

A. Whether that blessing be deny'd or giv'n,
Thus far was right, the rest belongs to Heav'n.

1. Arbuthnot had been physician to Queen Anne.

SATIRES AND EPISTLES OF HORACE
IMITATED

THE SECOND SATIRE OF THE SECOND
BOOK OF HORACE

TO MR BETHEL[1]

WHAT, and how great, the Virtue and the Art
To live on little with a chearful heart;
(A doctrine sage, but truly none of mine)
Let's talk, my friends, but talk before we dine;
Not when a gilt Buffet's reflected pride
Turns you from sound Philosophy aside;
Not when from plate to plate your eye-balls roll,
And the brain dances to the mantling bowl.

Hear BETHEL's Sermon, one not versed in schools,
But strong in sense, and wise without the rules.

Go, work, hunt, exercise! (he thus began)
Then scorn a homely dinner, if you can.
Your wine lock'd up, your Butler stroll'd abroad,
Or fish deny'd (the river yet unthaw'd),
If then plain bread and milk will do the feat,
The pleasure lies in you, and not the meat.

Preach as I please, I doubt our curious men
Will choose a pheasant still before a hen;
Yet hens of Guinea full as good I hold,
Except you eat the feathers green and gold.
Of carps and mullets why prefer the great,
(Tho' cut in pieces ere my Lord can eat)
Yet for small Turbots such esteem profess?
Because God made these large, the other less.

Oldfield,[2] with more than Harpy throat endu'd,
Cries, 'Send me, Gods! a whole Hog barbecu'd!'

1. Hugh Bethel (d. 1748), one of Pope's earliest friends.
2. A notable glutton who is supposed to have spent £1,500 a year
   on good food.

Oh, blast it, South-winds! till a stench exhale
Rank as the ripeness of a rabbit's tail.
By what Criterion do ye eat, d'ye think,
If this is priz'd for sweetness, that for stink?
When the tir'd glutton labours through a treat,
He finds no relish in the sweetest meat,
He calls for something bitter, something sour,
And the rich feast concludes extremely poor:
Cheap eggs, and herbs, and olives still we see;
Thus much is left of old Simplicity!

    The Robin-red-breast till of late had rest,
And children sacred held a Martin's nest,
Till Beccaficos[1] sold so dev'lish dear
To one that was, or would have been, a Peer.
Let me extol a Cat, on oysters fed,
I'll have a party at the Bedford-head;[2]
Or ev'n to crack live Crawfish recommend;
I'd never doubt at Court to make a friend.

    'Tis yet in vain, I own, to keep a pother
About one vice, and fall into the other:
Between Excess and Famine lies a mean;
Plain, but not sordid; tho' not splendid, clean.

    Avidien, or his Wife (no matter which,
For him you'll call a dog, and her a bitch)
Sell their presented partridges, and fruits,
And humbly live on rabbits and on roots:
One half-pint bottle serves them both to dine,
And is at once their vinegar and wine.
But on some lucky day (as when they found
A lost Bank-bill, or heard their Son was drown'd)
At such a feast, old vinegar to spare,
Is what two souls so gen'rous cannot bear:

1. The Italian name for a small migratory bird.
2. A famous eating-house. *P.*

Oil, tho' it stink, they drop by drop impart,
But sowse the cabbage with a bounteous heart.

He knows to live, who keeps the middle state,
And neither leans on this side, nor on that;
Nor stops, for one bad cork, his butler's pay;
Swears, like Albutius, a good cook away;
Nor lets, like Naevius, ev'ry error pass,
The musty wine, foul cloth, or greasy glass.

Now hear what blessings Temperance can bring:
(Thus said our Friend, and what he said I sing)
First Health: The stomach (cramm'd from ev'ry dish,
A tomb of boil'd and roast, and flesh and fish,
Where bile, and wind, and phlegm, and acid jar,
And all the man is one intestine war)
Remembers oft the School-boy's simple fare,
The temp'rate sleeps, and spirits light as air.

How pale each Worshipful and Rev'rend guest
Rise from a Clergy or a City feast!
What life in all that ample body, say?
What heav'nly particle inspires the clay?
The Soul subsides, and wickedly inclines
To seem but mortal, ev'n in sound Divines.

On morning wings how active springs the Mind
That leaves the load of yesterday behind!
How easy ev'ry labour it pursues!
How coming to the Poet ev'ry Muse!
Not but we may exceed, some holy time,
Or tir'd in search of Truth, or search of Rhyme;
Ill health some just indulgence may engage,
And more the sickness of long life, Old age;
For fainting Age what cordial drop remains,
If our intemperate Youth the vessel drains?

Our fathers prais'd rank Ven'son. You suppose,
Perhaps, young men! our fathers had no nose.

Not so: a Buck was then a week's repast,
And 'twas their point, I ween, to make it last;
More pleas'd to keep it till their friends could come,
Than eat the sweetest by themselves at home.
Why had not I in those good times my birth,
Ere coxcomb-pies or coxcombs were on earth?

    Unworthy he, the voice of Fame to hear –
That sweetest music to an honest ear –
(For, faith, Lord Fanny! you are in the wrong,
The world's good word is better than a song,)
Who has not learn'd, fresh sturgeon and ham-pie
Are no rewards for want, and infamy!
When Luxury has lick'd up all thy pelf,
Curs'd by thy neighbours, thy trustees, thyself,
To friends, to fortune, to mankind a shame,
Think how posterity will treat thy name;
And buy a rope, that future times may tell
Thou hast at least bestow'd one penny well.

    'Right,' cries his Lordship, 'for a rogue in need
To have a Taste is insolence indeed:
In me 'tis noble, suits my birth and state,
My wealth unwieldy, and my heap too great.'
Then, like the Sun, let Bounty spread her ray,
And shine that superfluity away.
Oh Impudence of wealth! with all thy store,
How dar'st thou let one worthy man be poor?
Shall half the new-built churches round thee fall?
Make Quays, build Bridges, or repair Whitehall:
Or to thy Country let that heap be lent,
As M**o's[1] was, but not at five per cent.

    Who thinks that Fortune cannot change her mind,
Prepares a dreadful jest for all mankind.

1. The Duchess of Marlborough was reported to lend money to the
Government at a great interest.

And who stands safest? tell me, is it he
That spreads and swells in puff'd Prosperity,
Or blest with little, whose preventing care
In peace provides fit arms against a war?

    Thus BETHEL spoke, who always speaks his thought,
And always thinks the very thing he ought:
His equal mind I copy what I can,
And as I love, would imitate the Man.
In South-Sea[1] days not happier, when surmis'd
The Lord of Thousands, than if now *Excis'd*;
In forest planted by a Father's hand,
Than in five acres now of rented land.
Content with little, I can piddle here
On brocoli and mutton, round the year;
But ancient friends (tho' poor, or out of play)
That touch my bell, I cannot turn away.
'Tis true, no Turbots dignify my boards,
But gudgeons, flounders, what my Thames affords:
To Hounslow-heath I point, and Bansted-down,
Thence comes your mutton, and these chicks my own:
From yon old walnut-tree a show'r shall fall;
And grapes, long ling'ring on my only wall,
And figs from standard and espalier join;
The Dev'l is in you if you cannot dine:
Then cheerful healths (your Mistress shall have
    place)
And, what's more rare, a Poet shall say Grace.

    Fortune not much of humbling me can boast;
Tho' double tax'd, how little have I lost?
My Life's amusements have been just the same,
Before and after Standing Armies came.
My lands are sold, my father's house is gone;
I'll hire another's; is not that my own,

1. See p. 153, n. 3.

And yours, my friends? through whose free-op'ning
    gate
None comes too early, none departs too late;
(For I, who hold sage Homer's rule the best,
Welcome the coming, speed the going guest).
'Pray Heav'n it last!' (cries SWIFT[1]) 'as you go on;
I wish to God this house had been your own:
Pity! to build, without a son or wife:
Why, you'll enjoy it only all your life.'
Well, if the use be mine, can it concern one,
Whether the name belong to Pope or Vernon?
What's *Property*, dear Swift? You see it alter
From you to me, from me to Peter Walter;[2]
Or, in a mortgage, prove a Lawyer's share;
Or, in a jointure, vanish from the heir;
Or in pure equity (the case not clear)
The Chanc'ry takes your rents for twenty year:
At best, it falls to some ungracious son,
Who cries, 'My father's damn'd, and all's my own.'
Shades, that to BACON could retreat afford,
Become the portion of a booby Lord;
And Helmsley, once proud Buckingham's[3] delight,
Slides to a Scriv'ner or a city Knight.
Let lands and houses have what Lords they will,
Let Us be fix'd, and our own masters still.

THE FIRST EPISTLE OF THE FIRST
BOOK OF HORACE

TO LORD BOLINGBROKE[1]

St John, whose love indulg'd my labours past,
Matures my present, and shall bound my last!
Why will you break the Sabbath of my days?
Now sick alike of Envy and of Praise.
Public too long, ah let me hide my Age!
See Modest Cibber[2] now has left the Stage:
Our Gen'rals now, retir'd to their Estates,
Hang their old Trophies o'er the Garden gates,
In Life's cool Ev'ning satiate of Applause,
Nor fond of bleeding, ev'n in Brunswick's cause.

   A Voice there is, that whispers in my ear,
('Tis Reason's voice, which sometimes one can hear)
'Friend Pope! be prudent, let your Muse take breath,
And never gallop Pegasus to death;
Lest, stiff and stately, void of fire or force,
You limp, like Blackmore on a Lord Mayor's horse.'[3]

   Farewell, then, Verse, and Love, and ev'ry Toy,
The Rhymes and Rattles of the Man or Boy;
What right, what true, what fit we justly call,
Let this be all my care – for this is All:
To lay this harvest up, and hoard with haste
What ev'ry day will want, and most, the last.

1. See p. 119, n. 1.   2. See p. 174, n. 1.
3. The fame of this heavy poet, however problematical elsewhere,
was universally received in the city of London. His versification is
here exactly described; stiff, and not strong; stately and yet dull,
like the sober and slow paced animal generally employed to mount
the Lord Mayor: and therefore here humorously opposed to
Pegasus. *P.*

But ask not, to what Doctors I apply;
Sworn to no Master, of no Sect am I:
As drives the storm, at any door I knock:
And house with Montaigne now, or now with Locke.
Sometimes a Patriot, active in debate,
Mix with the World, and battle for the State,
Free as young Lyttelton,[1] her Cause pursue,
Still true to Virtue, and as warm as true:
Sometimes with Aristippus, or St Paul,
Indulge my candor, and grow all to all;
Back to my native Moderation slide,
And win my way by yielding to the tide.

Long, as to him who works for debt, the day,
Long as the Night to her whose Love's away,
Long as the Year's dull circle seems to run,
When the brisk Minor pants for twenty-one:
So slow th' unprofitable moments roll,
That lock up all the Functions of my soul;
That keep me from myself; and still delay
Life's instant business to a future day:
That task, which, as we follow, or despise,
The eldest is a fool, the youngest wise.
Which done, the poorest can no wants endure;
And which not done, the richest must be poor.

Late as it is, I put myself to school,
And feel some comfort not to be a fool.
Weak though I am of limb, and short of sight,
Far from a Lynx, and not a Giant quite;
I'll do what Mead and Cheselden advise,[2]
To keep these limbs, and to preserve these eyes.
Not to go back, is somewhat to advance,
And men must walk at least before they dance.

1. George Lyttelton (1709–73); poet and politician.
2. Two well-known contemporary physicians.

Say, does thy blood rebel, thy bosom move
With wretched Av'rice, or as wretched Love?
Know, there are Words and Spells which can
    control
Between the Fits this Fever of the Soul:
Know, there are Rhymes, which, fresh and fresh
    apply'd,
Will cure the arrant'st Puppy of his Pride.
Be furious, envious, slothful, mad, or drunk,
Slave to a Wife, or Vassal to a Punk,
A Switz, a High-dutch, or a Low-dutch Bear;
All that we ask is but a patient Ear.

'Tis the first Virtue, Vices to abhor:
And the first Wisdom, to be Fool no more.
But to the world no bugbear is so great,
As want of Figure, and a small Estate.
To either India see the Merchant fly,
Scared at the spectre of pale Poverty!
See him, with pains of body, pangs of soul,
Burn through the Tropic, freeze beneath the Pole!
Wilt thou do nothing for a nobler end,
Nothing, to make Philosophy thy friend?
To stop thy foolish views, thy long desires,
And ease thy heart of all that it admires?

Here, Wisdom calls: 'Seek Virtue first, be bold!
As Gold to Silver, Virtue is to Gold.'
There, London's voice: 'Get Money, Money still!
And then let Virtue follow, if she will.'
This, this the saving doctrine, preach'd to all,
From low St James's up to high St Paul;
From him whose quill stands quiver'd at his ear,
To him who notches sticks[1] at Westminster.

---

1. Exchequer tallies; an old method of reckoning in the Exchequer.

Barnard[1] in spirit, sense, and truth abounds;
'Pray then, what wants he?' Fourscore thousand
  pounds;
A Pension, or such Harness for a slave
As Bug now has, and Dorimant would have.
Barnard, thou art a Cit, with all thy worth;
But Bug and D*l, their *Honours*, and so forth.

  Yet ev'ry child another song will sing,
'Virtue, brave boys! 'tis Virtue makes a King.'
True, conscious Honour is to feel no sin,
He's arm'd without that's innocent within;
Be this thy Screen, and this thy Wall of Brass;
Compar'd to this, a Minister's an Ass.

  And say, to which shall our applause belong,
This new Court-jargon, or the good old song?
The modern language of corrupted Peers,
Or what was spoke at Cressy and Poitiers?
Who counsels best? who whispers, 'Be but great,
With Praise or Infamy leave that to fate;
Get Place and Wealth, if possible, with grace;
If not, by any means get Wealth and Place.'
For what? to have a Box where Eunuchs sing,
And foremost in the Circle eye a King.
Or he, who bids thee face with steady view
Proud Fortune, and look shallow Greatness through:
And, while he bids thee, sets th' Example too?
If such a Doctrine, in St James's air,
Should chance to make the well-drest Rabble stare;
If honest S*z take scandal at a Spark,
That less admires the Palace than the Park:
Faith, I shall give the answer Reynard gave:
'I cannot like, dread sir, your Royal Cave:

1. Sir John Barnard (1685–1764); M.P. and Lord Mayor of London.

Because I see, by all the tracks about,
Full many a Beast goes in, but none comes out.'
Adieu to Virtue, if you're once a Slave:
Send her to Court, you send her to her grave.

   Well, if a King's a Lion, at the least
The People are a many-headed Beast:
Can they direct what measures to pursue,
Who know themselves so little what to do?
Alike in nothing but one Lust of Gold,
Just half the land would buy, and half be sold:
Their Country's Wealth our mightier Misers drain,
Or cross, to plunder Provinces, the Main;
The rest, some farm the Poor-box, some the Pews;
Some keep Assemblies, and would keep the Stews;
Some with fat Bucks on childless Dotards fawn;
Some win rich Widows by their Chine and Brawn;
While with the silent growth of ten per cent.,
In dirt and darkness, hundreds stink content.

   Of all these ways, if each pursues his own,
Satire, be kind, and let the wretch alone:
But show me one who has it in his pow'r
To act consistent with himself an hour.
Sir Job sail'd forth, the ev'ning bright and still,
'No place on earth' (he cry'd) 'like Greenwich hill?'
Up starts a Palace, lo, th' obedient base }
Slopes at its foot, the woods its sides embrace, }
The silver Thames reflects its marble face. }
Now let some whimsy, or that Dev'l within, }
Which guides all those who know not what they mean, }
But give the Knight (or give his Lady) spleen; }
'Away, away! take all your scaffolds down,
For Snug's the word: My dear! we'll live in Town.'

   At am'rous Flavio is the stocking thrown?
That very night he longs to lie alone.

POEMS OF ALEXANDER POPE

The Fool, whose Wife elopes some thrice a quarter,
For matrimonial solace dies a martyr.
Did ever Proteus, Merlin, any witch,
Transform themselves so strangely as the Rich?
Well, but the Poor – The Poor have the same itch;
They change their weekly Barber, weekly News,
Prefer a new Japanner to their shoes,
Discharge their Garrets, move their beds, and run
(They know not whither) in a Chaise and one;
They hire their sculler, and when once aboard,
Grow sick, and damn the climate – like a Lord.

You laugh, half Beau, half Sloven if I stand;
My wig all powder, and all snuff my band;
You laugh, if coat and breeches strangely vary,
White gloves, and linen worthy Lady Mary![1]
But when no Prelate's Lawn with hair-shirt lin'd
Is half so incoherent as my Mind,
When (each opinion with the next at strife,
One ebb and flow of follies all my life)
I plant, root up; I build, and then confound;
Turn round to square, and square again to round;
You never change one muscle of your face,
You think this Madness but a common case,
Nor once to Chanc'ry, nor to Hale[2] apply;
Yet hang your lip, to see a Seam awry!
Careless how ill I with myself agree,
Kind to my dress, my figure, not to Me.
Is this my Guide, Philosopher, and Friend?
This, he who loves me, and who ought to mend?
Who ought to make me (what he can, or none),
That Man divine whom Wisdom calls her own;

1. Lady Mary Wortley Montagu (1689–1762); authoress and wit,
beauty yet a sloven.
2. Dr Richard Hale (1670–1728); studied insanity.

Great without Title, without Fortune bless'd;
Rich ev'n when plunder'd, honour'd while oppress'd;
Lov'd without youth, and follow'd without pow'r;
At home, tho' exil'd; free, tho' in the Tow'r;
In short, that reas'ning, high, immortal Thing,
Just less than Jove, and much above a King,
Nay, half in heav'n – except (what's mighty odd)
A Fit of Vapours clouds this Demi-God.

FROM

THE FIRST EPISTLE OF THE SECOND
BOOK OF HORACE

TO AUGUSTUS

OF little use the Man you may suppose,
Who says in verse what others say in prose;
Yet let me show, a Poet's of some weight,
And (tho' no Soldier) useful to the State.
What will a Child learn sooner than a song?
What better teach a Foreigner the tongue?
What's long or short, each accent where to place,
And speak in public with some sort of grace?
I scarce can think him such a worthless thing,
Unless he praise some Monster of a King;
Or Virtue or Religion turn to sport,
To please a lewd or unbelieving Court.
Unhappy Dryden! – in all Charles's days,
Roscommon only boasts unspotted bays;
And in our own (excuse some Courtly stains)
No whiter page than Addison remains.
He from the taste obscene reclaims our youth,
And sets the Passions on the side of Truth,

Forms the soft bosom with the gentlest art,
And pours each human Virtue in the heart.
Let Ireland tell, how Wit upheld her cause,
Her Trade supported, and supplied her Laws;
And leave on SWIFT this grateful verse ingrav'd,
'The Rights a Court attack'd, a Poet sav'd.'
Behold the hand that wrought a Nation's cure,
Stretch'd to relieve the Idiot and the Poor,
Proud Vice to brand, or injur'd Worth adorn,
And stretch the Ray to Ages yet unborn.
Not but there are, who merit other palms;
Hopkins and Sternhold glad the heart with psalms:
The Boys and Girls whom Charity maintains,
Implore your help in these pathetic strains:
How could Devotion touch the country pews,
Unless the Gods bestow'd a proper Muse?
Verse cheers their leisure, Verse assists their work,
Verse prays for Peace, or sings down Pope and Turk.
The silenc'd Preacher yields to potent strain,
And feels that Grace his pray'r besought in vain;
The blessing thrills through all the lab'ring throng,
And Heav'n is won by Violence of Song.

FROM THE

EPILOGUE TO THE SATIRES

THE PROGRESS OF VICE

VIRTUE may choose the high or low Degree,
'Tis just alike to Virtue, and to me;
Dwell in a Monk, or light upon a King,
She's still the same belov'd, contented thing.
Vice is undone, if she forgets her Birth,
And stoops from Angels to the Dregs of Earth:
But 'tis the *Fall* degrades her to a Whore;
Let *Greatness* own her, and she's mean no more;
Her Birth, her Beauty, Crowds and Courts confess,
Chaste Matrons praise her, and grave Bishops bless;
In golden Chains the willing World she draws,
And hers the Gospel is, and hers the Laws,
Mounts the Tribunal, lifts her scarlet head,
And sees pale Virtue carted in her stead.
Lo! at the wheels of her Triumphal Car,
Old England's Genius, rough with many a Scar,
Dragg'd in the dust! his arms hang idly round,
His Flag inverted trails along the ground!
Our Youth, all liv'ry'd o'er with foreign Gold,
Before her dance: behind her, crawl the Old!
See thronging Millions to the Pagod run,
And offer Country, Parent, Wife, or Son!
Hear her black Trumpet through the Land proclaim,
That NOT TO BE CORRUPTED IS THE SHAME!
In Soldier, Churchman, Patriot, Man in Pow'r,
'Tis Av'rice all, Ambition is no-more!
See, all our Nobles begging to be Slaves!
See, all our Fools aspiring to be Knaves!

The Wit of Cheats, the Courage of a Whore,
Are what ten thousand envy and adore!
All, all look up with reverential Awe,
At Crimes that 'scape, or triumph o'er the Law:
While Truth, Worth, Wisdom, daily they decry –
'Nothing is Sacred now but Villany.'

  Yet may this Verse (if such a Verse remain)
Show, there was one who held it in disdain.

INDEX OF FIRST LINES

A pleasing Form; a firm, yet cautious Mind   91
A shepherd's Boy (he seeks no better name)   4
As some fond Virgin, whom her mother's care   84
Awake, my St John! leave all meaner things   119

Begone, ye critics, and restrain your spite   98
Beneath the shade a spreading Beech displays   7

Come then, my friend, my Genius! come along   129

First in these fields I try the sylvan strains   1

Happy the man, whose wish and care   93
Heav'n from all creatures hides the book of Fate   119
Hector, this heard, return'd without Delay   104
Here rests a Woman, good without pretence   91

I am His Highness' dog at Kew   101
I know the thing that's most uncommon   103
In these deep solitudes and awful cells   66
In these gay thoughts the Loves and Graces shine   81

Know then thyself, presume not God to scan   121

Nature and Nature's Laws lay hid in Night   92
Nothing so true as what you once let fall   139

Of little use the Man you may suppose   197
Of Manners gentle, of Affections mild   92
Oh be thou blest with all that Heav'n can send   102
Oh happiness! our being's end and aim   123
O Muse! relate (for you can tell alone   117

St John, whose love indulg'd my labours past   191
Shut, shut the door, good John! fatigu'd, I said   171
Silence! coeval with Eternity   94
Such were the notes thy once-lov'd Poet sung   89

The Troops exulting sate in order round   109
This Verse be thine, my friend, nor thou refuse   86
Thus having said, the Father of the Fires   109
Thus, near the gates conferring as they drew   115
Thyrsis, the music of that murm'ring spring   10

201

'Tis hard to say, if greater want of skill   14
'Tis strange, the Miser should his Cares employ   163
To this sad shrine, whoe'er thou art! draw near   91
To wake the soul by tender strokes of art   99

Virtue may choose the high or low Degree   199
Vital spark of heav'nly flame   97

What, and how great, the Virtue and the Art   185
What beck'ning ghost, along the moon-light shade   78
What dire offence from am'rous causes springs   40
Whate'er the Passion, knowledge, fame or pelf   122
What nothing earthly gives, or can destroy   124
While thus I stood, intent to see and hear   65
Who shall decide, when Doctors disagree   148

Yes, you despise the man to Books confined   130
Ye vig'rous swains! while youth ferments your blood   36

FOR THE BEST IN PAPERBACKS, LOOK FOR THE 🐧

In every corner of the world, on every subject under the sun, Penguin represents quality and variety – the very best in publishing today.

For complete information about books available from Penguin – including Puffins, Penguin Classics and Arkana – and how to order them, write to us at the appropriate address below. Please note that for copyright reasons the selection of books varies from country to country.

In the United Kingdom: Please write to *Dept E.P., Penguin Books Ltd, Harmondsworth, Middlesex, UB7 0DA.*

If you have any difficulty in obtaining a title, please send your order with the correct money, plus ten per cent for postage and packaging, to *PO Box No 11, West Drayton, Middlesex*

In the United States: Please write to *Dept BA, Penguin, 299 Murray Hill Parkway, East Rutherford, New Jersey 07073*

In Canada: Please write to *Penguin Books Canada Ltd, 2801 John Street, Markham, Ontario L3R 1B4*

In Australia: Please write to the *Marketing Department, Penguin Books Australia Ltd, P.O. Box 257, Ringwood, Victoria 3134*

In New Zealand: Please write to the *Marketing Department, Penguin Books (NZ) Ltd, Private Bag, Takapuna, Auckland 9*

In India: Please write to *Penguin Overseas Ltd, 706 Eros Apartments, 56 Nehru Place, New Delhi, 110019*

In the Netherlands: Please write to *Penguin Books Nederland B.V., Postbus 195, NL–1380AD Weesp*

In West Germany: Please write to *Penguin Books Ltd, Friedrichstrasse 10–12, D–6000 Frankfurt/Main 1*

In Spain: Please write to *Longman Penguin España, Calle San Nicolas 15, E–28013 Madrid*

In Italy: Please write to *Penguin Italia s.r.l., Via Como 4, I-20096 Pioltello (Milano)*

In France: Please write to *Penguin Books Ltd, 39 Rue de Montmorency, F–75003 Paris*

In Japan: Please write to *Longman Penguin Japan Co Ltd, Yamaguchi Building, 2–12–9 Kanda Jimbocho, Chiyoda-Ku, Tokyo 101*

FOR THE BEST IN PAPERBACKS, LOOK FOR THE

PENGUIN REFERENCE BOOKS

The New Penguin English Dictionary

Over 1,000 pages long and with over 68,000 definitions, this cheap, compact and totally up-to-date book is ideal for today's needs. It includes many technical and colloquial terms, guides to pronunciation and common abbreviations.

The Penguin Spelling Dictionary

What are the plurals of *octopus* and *rhinoceros*? What is the difference between *stationary* and *stationery*? And how about *annex* and *annexe*, *agape* and *Agape*? This comprehensive new book, the fullest spelling dictionary now available, provides the answers.

Roget's Thesaurus of English Words and Phrases   Betty Kirkpatrick (ed.)

This new edition of Roget's classic work, now brought up to date for the nineties, will increase anyone's command of the English language. Fully cross-referenced, it includes synonyms of every kind (formal or colloquial, idiomatic and figurative) for almost 900 headings. It is a must for writers and utterly fascinating for any English speaker.

The Penguin Dictionary of Quotations

A treasure-trove of over 12,000 new gems and old favourites, from Aesop and Matthew Arnold to Xenophon and Zola.

The Penguin Wordmaster Dictionary
Martin H. Manser and Nigel D. Turton

This dictionary puts the pleasure back into word-seeking. Every time you look at a page you get a bonus – a panel telling you everything about a particular word or expression. It is, therefore, a dictionary to be read as well as used for its concise and up-to-date definitions.

FOR THE BEST IN PAPERBACKS, LOOK FOR THE

PENGUIN REFERENCE BOOKS

The Penguin Guide to the Law

This acclaimed reference book is designed for everyday use and forms the most comprehensive handbook ever published on the law as it affects the individual.

The Penguin Medical Encyclopedia

Covers the body and mind in sickness and in health, including drugs, surgery, medical history, medical vocabulary and many other aspects. 'Highly commendable' – *Journal of the Institute of Health Education*

The Slang Thesaurus

Do you make the public bar sound like a gentleman's club? Do you need help in understanding *Minder*? The miraculous *Slang Thesaurus* will liven up your language in no time. You won't Adam and Eve it! A mine of funny, witty, acid and vulgar synonyms for the words you use every day.

The Penguin Dictionary of Troublesome Words   Bill Bryson

Why should you avoid discussing the *weather conditions*? Can a married woman be *celibate*? Why is it eccentric to talk about the *aroma* of a cowshed? A straightforward guide to the pitfalls and hotly disputed issues in standard written English.

A Dictionary of Literary Terms

Defines over 2,000 literary terms (including lesser known, foreign language and technical terms), explained with illustrations from literature past and present.

The Concise Cambridge Italian Dictionary

Compiled by Barbara Reynolds, this work is notable for the range of examples provided to illustrate the exact meaning of Italian words and phrases. It also contains a pronunciation guide and a reference grammar.

FOR THE BEST IN PAPERBACKS, LOOK FOR THE 🐧

PENGUIN CLASSICS

John Aubrey	**Brief Lives**
Francis Bacon	**The Essays**
George Berkeley	**Principles of Human Knowledge** and **Three Dialogues between Hylas and Philionous**
James Boswell	**The Life of Johnson**
Sir Thomas Browne	**The Major Works**
John Bunyan	**The Pilgrim's Progress**
Edmund Burke	**Reflections on the Revolution in France**
Thomas de Quincey	**Confessions of an English Opium Eater**
	Recollections of the Lakes and the Lake Poets
Daniel Defoe	**A Journal of the Plague Year**
	Moll Flanders
	Robinson Crusoe
	Roxana
	A Tour Through the Whole Island of Great Britain
Henry Fielding	**Jonathan Wild**
	Joseph Andrews
	The History of Tom Jones
Oliver Goldsmith	**The Vicar of Wakefield**
Richard Gough	**The History of Myddle**

FOR THE BEST IN PAPERBACKS, LOOK FOR THE 🐧

PENGUIN CLASSICS

William Hazlitt	**Selected Writings**
Thomas Hobbes	**Leviathan**
Samuel Johnson/ James Boswell	**A Journey to the Western Islands of Scotland** and **The Journal of a Tour to the Hebrides**
Charles Lamb	**Selected Prose**
Samuel Richardson	**Clarissa**
	Pamela
Richard Brinsley Sheridan	**The School for Scandal and Other Plays**
Adam Smith	**The Wealth of Nations**
Tobias Smollett	**The Expedition of Humphry Clinker**
	The Life and Adventures of Sir Launcelot Greaves
Richard Steele and Joseph Addison	Selections from the **Tatler** and the **Spectator**
Laurence Sterne	**The Life and Opinions of Tristram Shandy, Gentleman**
	A Sentimental Journey Through France and Italy
Jonathan Swift	**Gulliver's Travels**
Sir John Vanbrugh	**Four Comedies**